Englands

HELICON

edited
from the edition of 1600
with additional poems
from the edition
of 1614

by

HUGH MACDONALD

LONDON

ROUTLEDGE AND KEGAN PAUL LTD

First published in the Muses' Library in 1949
by Routledge and Kegan Paul Ltd
68–74 Carter Lane, London E.C.4
Printed in Great Britain
by Butler and Tanner Limited
Frome and London

*Owing to production delays
this book was not published
until 1950*

CONTENTS

INTRODUCTION BY HUGH MACDONALD   *page* xv

TO HIS LOVING KINDE FRIEND MAISTER JOHN
   BODENHAM   XXV

TO HIS VERY LOVING FRIENDS, M. NICHOLAS
   WANTON, AND M. GEORGE FAUCET   XXVi

TO THE READER, IF INDIFFERENT   XXVii

THE SHEEPHEARD TO HIS CHOSEN NIMPH
   S. Phil. Sidney   1

THEORELLO, A SHEEPHEARDS EDILLION *E. B.*   3

ASTROPHELS LOVE IS DEAD *Sir Phil. Sidney*   7

A PALINODE *E. B.*   8

ASTROPHELL THE SHEEP-HEARD, HIS COM-
   PLAINT TO HIS FLOCKE *S. Phil. Sidney*   9

HOBBINOLLS DITTIE IN PRAYSE OF ELIZA
   QUEENE OF THE SHEEPHEARDS *Edm. Spencer*   11

THE SHEEPHEARDS DAFFADILL *Michaell Drayton*   15

A CANZON PASTORALL IN HONOUR OF HER
   MAJESTIE *Edmund Bolton*   17

MELICERTUS MADRIGALE *Ro. Greene*   18

OLDE DAMONS PASTORALL *Thom. Lodge*   19

PERIGOT AND CUDDIES ROUNDELAY *Edm.
   Spencer*   20

PHILLIDA AND CORIDON *N. Breton*   23

TO COLIN CLOUTE *Sheepheard Tonie*   24

ROWLANDS SONG IN PRAISE OF THE FAIREST
   BETA *Mich. Drayton*   24

THE BARGINET OF ANTIMACHUS *Thom. Lodge*   28

MENAPHONS ROUNDELAY *Ro. Greene*   30

A PASTORALL OF PHILLIS AND CORIDON
   N. Breton   31

CORIDON AND MELAMPUS SONG *Geo. Peele* page 32

TITYRUS TO HIS FAIRE PHILLIS *J. D.* 32

SHEEPHEARD *J. M.* 33

ANOTHER OF THE SAME AUTHOUR *J. M.* 33

MENAPHON TO PESANA *Ro. Greene* 35

A SWEETE PASTORALL *N. Breton* 35

HARPALUS COMPLAYNT ON PHILLIDAES LOVE
BESTOWED ON CORIN, WHO LOVED HER NOT,
AND DENYED HIM THAT LOVED HER
L. T. Haward, Earl of Surrie 37

ANOTHER OF THE SAME SUBJECT, BUT MADE
AS IT WERE IN AUNSWERE *Shep. Tonie* 40

THE NIMPHES MEETING THEIR MAY QUEENE,
ENTERTAINE HER WITH THIS DITTIE
Tho. Watson 44

COLIN CLOUTES MOURNFULL DITTIE FOR THE
DEATH OF ASTROPHELL *Edm. Spencer* 44

DAMÆTAS JIGGE IN PRAISE OF HIS LOVE *John
Wootton* 45

MONTANUS PRAISE OF HIS FAIRE PHÆBE *Thom.
Lodge* 46

THE COMPLAINT OF THESTILIS THE FORSAKEN
SHEEPHEARD *L. T. Howard, E. of Surrie* 48

TO PHILLIS THE FAIRE SHEEPHEARDESSE *S. E. D.* 49

THE SHEEPHEARD DORONS JIGGE *Ro. Greene* 50

ASTROPHELL HIS SONG OF PHILLIDA AND
CORIDON *N. Breton* 51

THE PASSIONATE SHEEPHEARDS SONG
W. Shakespeare 53

THE UNKNOWNE SHEEPHEARDS COMPLAINT
Ignoto 54

ANOTHER OF THE SAME SHEEPHEARDS *Ignoto* 55

THE SHEEPHEARDS ALLUSION OF HIS OWNE
AMOROUS INFELICITIE, TO THE OFFENCE OF
ACTÆON *Tho. Watson* 56

vi

MONTANUS SONNET TO HIS FAIRE PHÆBE
  Thom. Lodge   page 57
PHÆBES SONNET, A REPLIE TO MONTANUS
  PASSION *Thom. Lodge*   58
CORIDONS SUPPLICATION TO PHILLIS
  N. Breton   59
DAMÆTAS MADRIGALL IN PRAISE OF HIS
  DAPHNIS *J. Wootton*   60
DORONS DESCRIPTION OF HIS FAIRE SHEEP-
  HEARDESSE SAMELA *Ro. Greene*   62
WODENFRIDES SONG IN PRAISE OF AMARGANA
  W. H.   63
ANOTHER OF THE SAME *W. H.*   64
AN EXCELLENT PASTORALL DITTIE *Shep. Tonie* 66
PHILLIDAES LOVE-CALL TO HER CORIDON,
  AND HIS REPLYING *Ignoto*   68
THE SHEEPHEARDS SOLACE *Tho. Watson*   70
SYRENUS SONG TO EUGERIUS *Bar. Yong*   70
THE SHEEPHEARD ARSILEUS REPLIE TO SYRE-
  NUS SONG *Bar. Yong*   73
A SHEEPHEARDS DREAME *N. Breton*   76
THE SHEEPHEARDS ODE *Rich. Barnefielde*   77
THE SHEEPHEARDS COMMENDATION OF HIS
  NIMPH *Earle of Oxenford*   79
CORIDON TO HIS PHILLIS *S. E. Dyer*   81
THE SHEEPHEARDS DESCRIPTION OF LOVE
  Ignoto   82
TO HIS FLOCKS *H. C.*   83
A ROUNDELAY BETWEEN TWO SHEEPHEARDS
  Mich. Drayton   84
THE SOLITARIE SHEEPHEARDS SONG *Thom.
  Lodge*   85
THE SHEEPHEARDS RESOLUTION IN LOVE *Tho.
  Watson*   85

CORIDONS HYMNE IN PRAISE OF AMARILLIS
  T. B.   page 86
THE SHEEPHEARD CARILLO HIS SONG Bar.
  Yong   87
CORINS DREAME OF HIS FAIRE CHLORIS W. S.   90
THE SHEEPHEARD DAMONS PASSION Thom.
  Lodge   91
THE SHEEPHEARD MUSIDORUS HIS COMPLAINT
  S. Phil. Sidney   91
THE SHEEPHEARDS BRAULE, ONE HALFE
  AUNSWERING THE OTHER S. Phil. Sidney   92
DORUS HIS COMPARISONS S. Phil. Sidney   92
THE SHEEPHEARD FAUSTUS HIS SONG Bar.
  Yong   93
ANOTHER OF THE SAME, BY FIRMIUS THE
  SHEEPHEARD Bar. Yong   95
DAMELUS SONG TO HIS DIAPHENIA H. C.   96
THE SHEEPHEARD EURYMACHUS TO HIS FAIRE
  SHEEPHEARDESSE MIRIMIDA Ro. Greene   97
THE SHEEPHEARD FIRMIUS HIS SONG Bar. Yong   99
THE SHEEPHEARDS PRAISE OF HIS SACRED
  DIANA   101
THE SHEEPHEARDS DUMPE S. E. D.   102
THE NIMPH DIANAES SONG Bar. Yong   103
ROWLANDS MADRIGALL Mich. Drayton   105
ALANIUS THE SHEEPHEARD, HIS DOLEFULL
  SONG, COMPLAYNING OF ISMENIAES CRUEL-
  TIE Bar. Yong   107
MONTANA THE SHEEPHEARD, HIS LOVE TO
  AMINTA Shep. Tonie   109
THE SHEEPHEARDS SORROW FOR HIS PHÆBES
  DISDAINE Ignoto   109
ESPILUS AND THERION, THEIR CONTENTION
  IN SONG FOR THE MAY-LADIE
  S. Phil. Sidney   111

OLDE MELIBEUS SONG, COURTING HIS
   NIMPH *Ignoto*   *page* 112
THE SHEEPHEARD SYLVANUS HIS SONG *Bar.*
   Yong   113
CORIDONS SONG *Thom. Lodge*   113
THE SHEEPHEARDS SONNET *Rich. Barnefielde* 115
SELVAGIA AND SILVANUS, THEIR SONG TO
   DIANA *Bar. Yong*   116
MONTANUS HIS MADRIGALL *Ro. Greene* 117
ASTROPHELL TO STELLA, HIS THIRD SONG
   S. Phil. Sidney   119
A SONG BETWEENE SYRENUS AND SYLVANUS
   Bar. Yong   120
CERES SONG IN EMULATION OF CINTHIA 122
A PASTORALL ODE TO AN HONOURABLE
   FRIEND *E. B.*   123
A NIMPHS DISDAINE OF LOVE *Ignoto* 124
APOLLOS LOVE-SONG FOR FAIRE DAPHNE 125
THE SHEEPHEARD DELICIUS HIS DITTIE *Bar.*
   Yong   125
AMINTAS FOR HIS PHILLIS *Tho. Watson* 127
FAUSTUS AND FIRMIUS SING TO THEIR NIMPH
   BY TURNES *Bar. Yong*   130
SIRENO A SHEEPHEARD, HAVING A LOCK OF
   HIS FAIRE NIMPHS HAIRE, WRAPT ABOUT
   WITH GREENE SILKE, MOURNES THUS IN A
   LOVE-DITTIE *Translated by S. Phil. Sidney,*
   out of Diana of Montmaior   131
A SONG BETWEENE TAURISIUS AND DIANA,
   AUNSWERING VERSE FOR VERSE *Bar. Yong* 133
ANOTHER SONG BEFORE HER MAJESTIE AT OX-
   FORD, SUNG BY A COMELY SHEEPHEARD,
   ATTENDED ON BY SUNDRIE OTHER SHEEP-
   HEARDS AND NIMPHS *Anonimus*   134

THE SHEEPHEARDS SONG: A CAROLL OR
HIMNE FOR CHRISTMAS *E. B.*   *page* 135

ARSILEUS HIS CAROLL, FOR JOY OF THE NEW
MARIAGE, BETWEENE SYRENUS AND DIANA
Bar. Yong   136

PHILISTUS FAREWELL TO FALSE CLORINDA
Out of M. Morleyes Madrigalls   139

ROSALINDES MADRIGALL *Thom. Lodge*   139

A DIALOGUE SONG BETWEENE SYLVANUS AND
ARSILIUS *Bar. Yong*   141

MONTANUS SONNET *S. E. D.*   142

THE NYMPH SELVAGIA HER SONG *Bar. Yong*   143

THE HEARD-MANS HAPPIE LIFE *Out of M.
Birds set Songs*   144

CINTHIA THE NIMPH, HER SONG TO FAIRE
POLYDORA *Bar. Yong*   145

THE SHEEPHEARD TO THE FLOWERS *Ignoto*   147

THE SHEEPHEARD ARSILIUS, HIS SONG TO HIS
REBECK *Bar. Yong*   149

ANOTHER OF ASTROPHELL TO HIS STELLA
S. Phil. Sidney   151

SYRENUS HIS SONG TO DIANAES FLOCKS *Bar.
Yong*   154

TO AMARILLIS *Out of M. Birds set Songs*   155

CARDENIA THE NIMPH, TO HER FALSE SHEEP-
HEARD FAUSTUS *Bar. Yong*   156

OF PHILLIDA *Out of M. Birds set Songs*   158

MELISEA HER SONG, IN SCORNE OF HER SHEEP-
HEARD NARCISSUS *Bar. Yong*   159

HIS AUNSWERE TO THE NIMPHS SONG *Bar.
Yong*   159

HER PRESENT AUNSWERE AGAINE TO HIM *Bar.
Yong*   160

HIS LAST REPLIE *Bar. Yong*   161

x

PHILON THE SHEEPHEARD, HIS SONG *Out of M. Birds set Songs* *page* 162

LYCORIS THE NIMPH, HER SAD SONG *Out of M. Morleyes Madrigalls* 163

TO HIS FLOCKS 163

TO HIS LOVE *Out of Maister John Dowlands booke of tableture for the Lute* 164

ANOTHER OF HIS CINTHIA *Out of Maister John Dowlands booke of tableture for the Lute* 165

ANOTHER TO HIS CINTHIA *Out of Maister John Dowlands booke of tableture for the Lute* 166

MONTANUS SONNET IN THE WOODS *S. E. D.* 167

THE SHEEPHEARDS SORROW, BEING DISDAINED IN LOVE *Thom. Lodge* 168

A PASTORALL SONG BETWEENE PHILLIS AND AMARILLIS, TWO NIMPHES, EACH AUNSWERING OTHER LINE FOR LINE *H. C.* 171

THE SHEEPHEARDS ANTHEME *Mich. Drayton* 173

THE COUNTESSE OF PEMBROOKES PASTORALL *Shep. Tonie* 174

ANOTHER OF ASTROPHELL *S. Phil. Sidney* 176

FAIRE PHILLIS AND HER SHEEPHEARD *I. G.* 177

THE SHEEPHEARDS SONG OF VENUS AND ADONIS *H. C.* 180

THIRSIS THE SHEEPHEARD HIS DEATHS SONG *Out of Maister N. Young his Musica Transalpina* 184

ANOTHER STANZA ADDED AFTER 185

ANOTHER SONET THENCE TAKEN 185

THE SHEEPHEARDS SLUMBER *Ignoto* 186

'IN WONTED WALKS' *S. Phil. Sidney* 190

OF DISDAINFULL DAPHNE *M. H. Nowell* 190

THE PASSIONATE SHEEPHEARD TO HIS LOVE *Chr. Marlow* 192

THE NIMPHS REPLY TO THE SHEEPHEARD *Ignoto* 193

xi

ANOTHER OF THE SAME NATURE, MADE
SINCE *Ignoto*   page 194
THE WOOD-MANS WALKE *Shep. Tonie*   195
THIRSIS THE SHEEPHEARD, TO HIS PIPE *Ignoto* 198
AN EXCELLENT SONNET OF A NIMPH *S. Phil.
Sidney*   199
A REPORT SONG IN A DREAME, BETWEENE A
SHEEPHEARD AND HIS NIMPH *N. Breton*   199
ANOTHER OF THE SAME *N. Breton*   200
THE SHEEPHEARDS CONCEITE OF PROMETHEUS
S. E. D.   201
ANOTHER OF THE SAME *S. Phil. Sidney*   201
THE SHEEPHEARDS SUNNE *Shep. Tonie*   202
COLIN THE ENAMOURED SHEEPHEARD, SING-
ETH THIS PASSION OF LOVE *Geo. Peele*   204
OENONES COMPLAINT IN BLANKE VERSE *Geo.
Peele*   205
THE SHEEPHEARDS CONSORT *Out of Ma.
Morleys Madrigals*   206

ADDITIONAL POEMS FROM
ENGLANDS HELICON 1614

AN INVECTIVE AGAINST LOVE *Ignoto*   209
DISPRAISE OF LOVE, AND LOVERS FOLLIES
Ignoto   210
TWO PASTORALS, UPON THREE FRIENDS
MEETING *S. Phil. Sidney*   211
AN HEROICALL POEME *Ignoto*   213
THE LOVERS ABSENCE KILS ME, HER PRESENCE
KILS ME *Ignoto*   215
LOVE THE ONLY PRICE OF LOVE *Ignoto*   216
THYRSIS PRAISE OF HIS MISTRESSE *W. Browne* 217
A DEFIANCE TO DISDAINEFULL LOVE *Ignoto* 219

AN EPITHALAMIUM; OR A NUPTIALL SONG,
APPLIED TO THE CEREMONIES OF MARRIAGE
Christopher Brooke *page* 219

NOTES   227
INDEX OF AUTHORS   253
INDEX OF FIRST LINES   255

INTRODUCTION

BY

HUGH MACDONALD

OF the many collections of lyrical poetry published between *Songes and Sonettes, written by the ryght honorable Lorde Henry Haward late Earle of Surrey, and other* in 1557, commonly known as *Tottels Miscellany*,[1] and *The Golden Treasury* in 1861, *Englands Helicon* is the most attractive. The general level of the poetry in the volume is high, and it includes several poems which are among the permanent treasures of English literature.

The books of the Madrigalists and the Lutenists contain a large number of exquisite poems. Many of them are more to our taste than some of the verse in *Englands Helicon*; but these books are in a different category from what we usually mean by an anthology, if only for the reason that the lines had to be printed so as to accompany the music. The poems, in fact, can only be read with comfort when they have been rearranged.[2]

The seventeenth century was weak in anthologies of lyrical poetry. Volumes of political satires were common after the Restoration; and Tonson with Dryden as a literary adviser published a famous series of miscellanies from 1684 onwards. None of them contains much good lyrical verse. These miscellanies were essentially collections of contemporary poems, and there was little good lyrical verse to collect. When the 'Fourth Edition' of these six volumes was published in 1716 a change in taste was shown by the inclusion of 'L'Allegro', 'Il Penseroso'; and 'The Garden' and

---

[1] From Richard Tottel the publisher. Howard is spelt Haward on the title-page.

[2] Several of these poems were printed in *Englands Helicon*. Dr. E. H. Fellowes printed the *Song Books* in his *English Madrigal Verse 1588–1632* (1920).

other pieces by Marvell.[1] Probably Hobart Kemp's *Collection of Poems Written upon several Occasions By several Persons* (1672) comes nearest to our conception of a good anthology, as it included many poems by Sedley and other Court poets. Kemp's volume formed the basis of a series of collections which appeared at intervals until 1716, but it cannot be said that the quality improved as the series developed.[2]

It seems strange to us that such poets as Herbert, Vaughan, Crashaw, Herrick and their contemporaries were hardly used by anthologists till the nineteenth century. That Donne, Herbert, and to a lesser extent, Crashaw, were read in the second half of the seventeenth century we know from the number of editions of their poems which were published; but speaking generally our best lyrical poets were neglected, along with their Elizabethan predecessors, till well after 1800.

Nor was the eighteenth century better than the seventeenth so far as anthologies of the kind we are discussing are concerned. Good collections were made such as D. Lewis's two volumes of *Miscellaneous Poems* (1726 and 1730), but such lyrical poems as they contain are by contemporary writers whose poetry does not stand comparison with that of many of the earlier poets. Dodsley's *Collection of Poems by Several Hands* (1748–1758) are at their best in verse written in heroic couplets, apart from such a poem as Gray's *Elegy. The Poetical Calendar* (12 numbers, 1763) compiled by Francis Fawkes and William Woty includes Marlowe's 'Come live with me and be my love' and some poems by Raleigh, but the series is chiefly remarkable for the inclusion of several poems by Collins printed there for the first time. Of course the seventeenth- and eighteenth-century compilers of miscellanies were collecting the verse of their contemporaries just as the Elizabethan compilers had done—but there was not such good lyrical verse to be

[1] Too many pieces, good, bad and indifferent, are contained in these volumes to suggest that they were more than a publisher's venture.

[2] See the present writer's article on these miscellanies in *Essays and Studies Collected by Arundell Esdaile* (1941 for 1940).

collected if the poetry written between 1600 and 1650 was ignored.[1]

But to return to the Tudor anthologies. These came into existence as soon as there was lyrical poetry to be used for them.[2] *Tottels Miscellany* has survived in at least eight editions published between 1557 and 1587. It was followed in 1566 by *Very Pleasaunt Sonettes and Storyes in Myter* by Clement Robinson. No copy of this is extant, and it is known only in the form of *A Handefull of Pleasant Delites*, 1584.[3] This book is composed of ballads or, at least, poems which could be sung. *The Paradyce of Daynty Devyses*, containing poems by Richard Edwards, Lord Vaux, the Earl of Oxford, William Hunnis, Jasper Heywood and others appeared in 1576. It was very popular, and by 1606 had gone into at least ten editions. *A Gorgeous Gallery of Gallant Inventions* came out in 1578. It includes poems by Owen Roydon, Thomas Proctor (whose initials appear as the editor on the title-page), Thomas Churchyard, Thomas Howell, Clement Robinson and Jasper Heywood. This volume, like the *P. of D.D.*, is somewhat sententious in tone and the verse is of an obviously earlier period than that in *Englands Helicon*. *The Phœnix Nest* edited by an unidentified 'R S' and containing poems by Thomas Lodge, Nicholas Breton, Sir Walter Raleigh and others was published in 1593. *Englands Helicon* came next in 1600, and was reprinted with nine additional poems in 1614. The series ended with *Davisons Poetical Rapsody*—as it is always called —in 1602. This reached a fourth edition in 1621. Davison collected mainly unpublished verse; a good

[1] There was a large number of eighteenth-century miscellanies, but like those mentioned above, the lyrical poetry which they contain was rarely of a high order.

[2] I need hardly say that the collected editions of 'Chaucer' from 1532 onwards or *The Mirror for Magistrates* first published in 1559 do not come within this short survey, although they were of composite authorship. A few other volumes, such as *Brittons Bowre of Delights* (1591 and 1597) and *The Passionate Pilgrim* (1599), are only anthologies in so far as they include poems not by Breton or Shakespeare respectively.

[3] For the evidence of the relationship of the two books, see *A.H. of P.D.*, edited by H. E. Rollins (1924). This anthology was reprinted by E. Arber in 1878 (The English Scholars' Library).

deal of it is by a certain 'A W' who has not been identified.[1] Interest in these miscellanies was revived by literary antiquaries such as Sir Egerton Brydges, Joseph Haslewood, J. O. Halliwell-Phillipps and J. Payne Collier in the first half of the nineteenth century.[2]

All these were true anthologies, but there were also published certain volumes which can be better described as collections or dictionaries of quotations. Two of these *Politeuphuia or Wits Commonwealth* 1597, and *Wits Theater of the little World* 1599 consist of short prose extracts, or poetry printed as prose, and two, *Bel-vedére or the Garden of the Muses* and *Englands Parnassus*,[3] both published in 1600, of poetical passages of not more than a few lines taken from contemporary writers. These books concern us here only because of their connection with *Englands Helicon*.

The first edition of *Englands Helicon* is in quarto and was carefully printed and edited. It was entered on the *Stationers Register* on the 4th of August 1600:

> John fflasket. Entred for his copie under the
> hands of master Doctor Barlowe
> and the Wardens a book called
> *Englands Helicon* . . . vjd.

A second edition in octavo was published in 1614.[4]

It has been the invariable custom, so far as I know, to enter *Englands Helicon* under the name of John Bodenham in library catalogues. But the real editor was almost certainly Nicholas Ling. Bullen first suggested that the initials 'L. N.' at the end of the

---

[1] See note to p. 209.

[2] The reprints by Brydges, Haslewood and Collier are scarce. They have been superseded by A. H. Bullen's editions of *Englands Helicon* (1887 and 1899), his edition of *Davisons Poetical Rapsody* (1890), the present writer's editions of *E.H.* (1925) and *The P.N.* (1926). Those who need fuller notes must consult the editions of *A.H.* of *P.D.*, *The P.* of *D.D.*, *A.G.G.* of *G.I.*, *The P.N.*, *E.H.* and *D.P.R.* edited by H. E. Rollins between 1924 and 1935.

[3] Edited by C. Crawford (1913). This type of book continued to flourish as is shown by such volumes as Joshua Poole's *The English Parnassus* (1657) and the numerous editions of Edward Bysshe's *The Art of English Poetry* (1702).

[4] See p. 249.

address 'To the Reader' were those of Ling transposed. The late Dr. J. W. Hebel put forward the suggestion that Ling was the actual editor.[1] This has been accepted by Professor H. E. Rollins, and I have little doubt that this view is correct. John Bodenham obviously had a close connection with the anthology; but he was probably in the position of a patron rather than an editor, although it is, of course, impossible to know whether he did or did not indicate his preferences to Ling. Bodenham's arms (to which he may or may not have been entitled) are printed on the back of the title-leaf of the 1600 edition of *Englands Helicon*. On the page following are some verses by a certain 'A. B.', whose identity is not known, addressed 'To his Loving Kinde Friend Maister John Bodenham'. These verses refer to *Wits Commonwealth*, *Wits Theater* and *Belvedére or the Garden of the Muses*, which are linked by 'A. B.' with *Englands Helicon*. Ling is known to have edited *Politeuphuia or Wits Commonwealth* (1597), because he discusses his editorial methods in his prefaces to the first and second editions, and these prefaces are signed by him in a normal way. Moreover *Englands Helicon* contains five hitherto unpublished poems by Michael Drayton, and as Ling was for a time Drayton's publisher he is likely to have had access to Drayton's unpublished material. No satisfactory explanation has been offered as to why Nicholas Ling's initials should have been reversed. As the book was very carefully produced there is no reason to suppose that this was due to a printer's error. The dedication of Anthony Munday's play, *Fedele and Fortunio*, 1584 is signed 'M. A.' in some copies, but as others are signed 'A. M.' we are not, I think, carried much further.

Mention should be made that one of the preliminary sonnets before *Bel-vedére* calls Bodenham [2] the:

First causer and collector of these floures.

[1] *The Library*, September 1924.
[2] Information about John Bodenham and Nicholas Wanton to whom, with one George Faucet, 'A. B.' addresses the prose epistle was published by Dr. Franklin B. Williams in *Studies in Philology*, April 1934. Professor Rollins has given the gist of Dr. Williams's

But if he were the 'collector' of the pieces in *Belvedére* he was not necessarily the 'collector' of the poems in *Englands Helicon*.

'A. B.' can no doubt be dismissed as a possible editor, for he says: 'My paines heerin, I cannot terme it great'.

Whoever was responsible for the book [1] had a very definite object in view. He wished to make it a pastoral anthology, and to this end he went freely to such books as the *Arcadia*, Greene's *Menaphon* and Lodge's *Rosalynde* for his material. If the original titles to the poems did not suit his purpose, he supplied new ones, and he frequently made small changes in the poems themselves to give them the desired pastoral character. This preoccupation may explain the inclusion of so large a number of poems from Bartholomew Yong's *Diana*—a translation of a Spanish pastoral romance by Montemeyor. These poems have been the chief ground of criticism brought against *Englands Helicon*. I can only say that to me they seem to vary in merit.

An unusual feature of the book is the existence of small slips changing the original attribution to *Ignoto* in the case of four poems, and from Sir Philip Sidney to Nicholas Breton in the case of a fifth. I refer to these slips in my notes to the appropriate poems.

In the British Museum is a manuscript list (Harl.

---

discoveries in his notes to his edition of *Englands Helicon*. Nicholas Wanton was the youngest son of Thomas Wanton by his wife Joan, a niece of Sir William Laxton at one time Lord Mayor of London. Nicholas was born in 1544 and in 1571 was made free of the London Grocers Company. He was living in York in 1597. He gathered materials for a history of York and Yorkshire, part of which are in two manuscripts in the Bodleian (MSS. Rawl. B.450, B.451). He died in March 1618. In York Minster, there is a monument to him. Wanton's eldest sister, Katherine, married William Bodenham, a London grocer, and their first child was our John Bodenham who was born *c.* 1558. John Bodenham went to Merchant Taylors School in 1570. He was left a fortune by his father. He took no active part in the affairs of the Grocers Company. He was at York in 1600. He died in July 1610 (from Rollins, II, p. 67).

[1] C. Crawford in his introduction to *Englands Parneessus* concludes that Bodenham was the editor.

MS. 280, fo. 99–101) [1] believed to be in the handwriting of Francis Davison, giving the first lines of the poems in *Englands Helicon* and the names of the authors, so far as Davison thought he knew them. This list differs now and then from the book in its attributions, but it cannot be regarded as a reliable authority.

Of the 150 poems printed in the first edition more than three-quarters had appeared in books already published: of the 9 added in the 1614 edition 7 were from *Davisons Poetical Rapsody*.

It remains to explain my methods in editing this edition. It has been set up from a copy of my 1925 edition after I had carefully collated the text with Malone's copy in the Bodleian and with constant reference to the Crynes copy in the same library. I have also collated my 1925 text of the 9 additional poems with the copy of the 1614 edition in the British Museum. In my 1925 text I retained the *i* and *j* and *u* and *v* of the 1600 edition. I have here modernized the *u* and *v* throughout; and the *i* and *j* where the reader's attention might be held up: e.g. I have substituted *Joves* for *Ioues*. The use of these letters was a printer's convention [2] which was never consistent, and which had almost disappeared by the end of the first third of the seventeenth century. Moreover, it has been the long *ſ* rather than the *i* and *j* and *u* and *v* that has led to textual errors. There is a word on page 44, 'proud', which is of interest in this connection. I have let it stand as it was originally printed because it is a possible reading, but provd = prov'd is more likely to be correct. This instance tells for modernization, as an ideal editor ought to decide which word is intended. Apart from the above changes the spelling is that of the original texts.

I have not consciously departed from the original texts except where there seems to be a printer's error. I have recorded these in the footnotes. I have retained

[1] Cf. note to 'An Invective against Love', p. 209. Rollins reprints Harl. MS. 280, fos. 99–101. The list was made by turning over the pages of *E.H.* 1600; but as Davison had obviously read extensively, it cannot be ignored.

[2] See R. B. McKerrow's *An Introduction to Bibliography* (1927), pp. 310–12.

the original punctuation, because *Englands Helicon* is exceptionally well punctuated on the Elizabethan system. It has not been possible to reproduce Bodenham's coat-of-arms, or the decorations and rules of the first edition; I have thought it unnecessary to retain the full stops at the ends of headlines, titles of poems or the names of the authors. This again is a mere printing convention. The Muses' Library does not admit of a page-for-page reprint. I have not added textual notes, as it is tiresome, if not impossible, to build up the texts of the poems as they were originally written from such notes. I have, however, frequently given the best edited modern edition in my notes at the end of this book. I have generally given the date of the first edition of a book from which Ling took a poem, although in many cases he used a later edition. As Ling made alterations in the poems he used to suit the scheme of his book knowledge of the exact edition of the book he went to is not of great importance.

The editions of 1600 and 1614 are very rare books. There are copies of both in the British Museum; there are two copies of the 1600 edition in the Bodleian Library, one in the John Rylands Library at Manchester and two fragments in the University Library, Cambridge. As it is not possible for me to give the location of copies in America with complete certainty, I omit mention of the few there are.

Since my edition of 1925 was published a very elaborate edition, already referred to, in two volumes by my friend Professor H. E. Rollins of Harvard University has appeared. All who need more information than I have given must consult Professor Rollins's edition.

In conclusion it is only right that a modern editor of *Englands Helicon* should pay tribute to A. H. Bullen. Although somewhat slap-dash in his methods he was the real pioneer of the modern study of Elizabethan poetry. If I have not referred in more detail to his two editions of *Englands Helicon*, or to earlier reprints it is because all editions are now difficult to get. It was Bullen who did more than anyone else to ease the task of the two subsequent editors of this famous book.

ENGLANDS
HELICON.

Casta placent superis,
    pura cum veste venite,
Et manibus puris
    sumite fontis aquam.

AT LONDON
Printed by I. R. for *Iohn Flasket*, and are
to be sold in Paules Church-yard, at the signe
of the Beare. 1600.

TO
HIS LOVING KINDE FRIEND
Maister *John Bodenham*

WITS Common-wealth, the first fruites of thy paines,
    Drew on *Wits Theater,* thy second Sonne:
    By both of which, I cannot count the gaines,
    And wondrous profit that the world hath wonne.
Next, in the *Muses Garden,* gathering flowres,
    Thou mad'st a Nosegay, as was never sweeter:
    Whose sent will savour to Times latest bowres,
    And for the greatest Prince no Poesie meeter.
Now comes thy *Helicon,* to make compleate
    And furnish up thy last impos'd designe:
    My paines heerein, I cannot terme it great,
    But what-so-ere, my love (and all) is thine.
      Take love, take paines, take all remaines in me:
      And where thou art, my hart still lives with thee.
                          A. B.

To his very loving friends,
M. *Nicholas Wanton*, and M. *George Faucet*

THOUGH many miles (but more occasions) doo sunder us (kind Gentlemen) yet a promise at parting, dooth in justice claime performance, and assurance of gentle acceptance, would mightilie condemne me if I should neglect it. *Helicon*, though not as I could wish, yet in such good sort as time would permit, having past the pikes of the Presse, comes now to *Yorke* to salute her rightfull Patrone first, and next (as his deere friends and kindsmen) to offer you her kinde service. If shee speede well there, it is all shee requires, if they frowne at her heere, she greatly not cares: for the wise (shee knowes) will never be other then them selves, as for such then as would seeme so, but neither are, nor ever will be, she holds this as a maine principle; that their malice neede as little be feared, as their favour or friendship is to be desired. So hoping you will not forget us there, as we continuallie shall be mindefull of you heere. I leave you to the delight of *Englands Helicon*.

Yours in all he may,
A. B.

To the Reader, if indifferent

MANY honoured names have heretofore (in their particuler interest,) patronized some part of these inventions: many here be, that onely these Collections have brought to light, & not inferiour (in the best opinions) to anie before published. The travaile that hath beene taken in gathering them from so many handes, hath wearied some howres, which severed, might in part have perished, digested into this meane volume, may in the opinion of some not be altogether unworthy the labour. If any man hath beene defrauded of any thing by him composed, by another mans title put to the same, hee hath this benefit by this collection, freely to challenge his owne in publique, where els he might be robd of his proper due. No one thing beeing here placed by the Collector of the same under any mans name, eyther at large, or in letters, but as it was delivered by some especiall coppy comming to his handes. No one man, that shall take offence that his name is published to any invention of his, but he shall within the reading of a leafe or two, meete with another in reputation every way equal with himselfe, whose name hath beene before printed to his Poeme, which nowe taken away were more then theft: which may satisfie him that would faine seeme curious or be intreated for his fame.

Nowe, if any Stationer shall finde faulte, that his Coppies are robd by any thing in this Collection, let me aske him this question, Why more in this, then in any Divine or humaine Authour: From whence a man (writing of that argument) shal gather any saying, sentence, similie, or example, his name put to it who is the Authour of the same. This is the simplest of many reasons that could I urdge, though perhaps the neerest his capacitie, but that I would be loth to trouble my selfe, to satisfie him. Further, if any man whatsoever, in prizing of his owne birth or fortune, shall take in scorne, that a far meaner man in the eye of the world, shall be placed by him: I tell him plainly whatsoever so excepting, that, that mans wit is set by his, not that man by him. In which degree, the names of Poets (all feare and dutie ascribed to her great and sacred Name) have beene placed with the names of the greatest Princes of the world, by the most autentique and worthiest judgements, without disparagement to their soveraigne titles: which if any man taking exception thereat, in ignorance know not, I hold him unworthy to be placed by the meanest that is but graced with the title of a Poet. Thus gentle Reader I wish thee all happines.

L. N.

Englands

H E L I C O N

_____

The Sheepheard to his chosen Nimph

ONELY joy, now heere you are,
Fit to heare and ease my care:
Let my whispring voyce obtaine,
Sweet reward for sharpest paine.
    Take me to thee, and thee to me,
    No, no, no, no, my Deere, let be.

Night hath clos'd all in her cloke,
Twinkling starres Love-thoughts provoke,
Daunger hence good care dooth keepe,
Jealousie it selfe dooth sleepe.
    Take me to thee, and thee to me:
    No, no, no, no, my Deere, let be.

Better place no wit can finde,
Cupids yoake to loose or binde,
These sweet flowers on fine bed too,
Us in their best language woo,
    Take me to thee, and thee to me:
    No, no, no, no, my Deere, let be.

This small light the Moone bestowes,
Serves thy beames but to enclose,
So to raise my hap more hie,
Feare not else, none can us spie.
    Take me to thee, and thee to me:
    No, no, no, no, my Deare, let be.

That you heard was but a Mouse,
Dumbe sleepe holdeth all the house,
Yet a-sleepe me thinks they say,
Young folkes, take time while you may.
    Take me to thee, and thee to me:
    No, no, no, no, my Deare, let be.

Niggard Time threats, if we misse
This large offer of our blisse,
Long stay, ere he graunt the same,
(Sweet then) while each thing dooth frame,
    Take me to thee, and thee to me:
    No, no, no, no, my Deere, let be.

Your faire Mother is a bed,
Candles out, and Curtaines spred,
She thinks you doo Letters write,
Write, but let me first indite.
    Take me to thee, and thee to me,
    No, no, no, no, my Deere, let be.

Sweete (alas) why saine you thus?
Concord better fitteth us.
Leave to *Mars* the force of hands,
Your power in your beauty stands.
    Take me to thee, and thee to me:
    No, no, no, no, my Deare, let be.

Woe to me, and you doo sweare
Me to hate, but I forebeare,

Cursed be my destenies all,
That brought me to so high a fall.
    Soone with my death I will please thee:
    No, no, no, no, my Deare, let be.

S. Phil. Sidney

saine] obsolete form of *say*

Theorello

A Sheepheards Edillion

YOU Sheepheards which on hillocks sit
    like Princes in their throanes:
And guide your flocks, which else would flit,
    your flocks of little ones:
Good Kings have not disdained it,
    but Sheepheards have beene named:
A sheepe-hooke is a Scepter fit,
    for people well reclaimed.
The Sheepheards life so honour'd is and praised:
That Kings lesse happy seeme, though higher raised.

The Sommer Sunne hath guilded faire,
    with morning rayes the mountaines:
The birds doo caroll in the ayre,
    and naked Nimphs in Fountaines.
The *Silvanes* in their shagged haire,
    with *Hamadriades* trace:
The shadie *Satires* make a Quiere,
    which rocks with Ecchoes grace.
All breathe delight, all solace in the season:
Not now to sing, were enemie to reason.

Cosma my Love, and more then so,
    the life of mine affections:

3

Nor life alone, but Lady too,
    and Queene of their directions.
Cosma my Love, is faire you know,
    and which you Sheepheards know not:
Is (*Sophi* said) thence called so,
    but names her beauty showe not.
Yet hath the world no better name then she:
And then the world, no fairer thing can be.

The Sunne upon her fore-head stands,
    (or jewell Sunne-like glorious,)
Her fore-head wrought with *Joves* owne hands,
    for heavenly white notorious.
Her golden lockes like *Hermus* sands,
    (or then bright *Hermus* brighter:)
A spangled Cauill binds in with bands,
    then silver morning lighter.
And if the Planets are the chiefe in skies:
No other starres then Planets are her eyes.

Her cheeke, her lip, fresh cheeke, more fresh,
    then selfe-blowne buds of Roses:
Rare lip, more red then those of flesh,
    which thousand sweetes encloses:
Sweet breath, which all things dooth refresh,
    and words than breath farre sweeter:
Cheeke firme, lip firme, not fraile nor nesh,
    as substance which is fleeter.
In praise doo not surmount, although in placing:
Her christall necke, round breast, and armes em-
      bracing.

The thorough-shining ayre I weene,
    is not so perfect cleare:
As is the skie of her faire skinne,
    whereon no spots appeare.
The parts which ought not to be seene,
    for soveraigne woorth excell:

4

Her thighs with Azure braunched beene,
    and all in her are well.
Long Ivorie hands, legges straighter then the Pine:
Well shapen feete, but vertue most divine.

Nor cloathed like a Sheepheardesse,
    but rather like a Queene:
Her mantle dooth the formes expresse,
    of all which may be seene.
Roabe fitter for an Empresse,
    then for a Sheepheards love:
Roabe fit alone for such a Lasse,
    as Emperours doth move.
Roabe which heavens Queene, the bride of her owne
        brother,
Would grace herselfe with, or with such another.

Who ever (and who else but *Jove*)
    embroidered the same:
Hee knew the world, and what did move,
    in all the mightie frame.
So well (belike his skill to prove)
    the counterfeits he wrought:
Of wood-Gods, and of every groave,
    and all which else was ought.
Is there a beast, a bird, a fish worth noate?
Then that he drew, and picturde in her coate.

A vaile of Lawne like vapour thin
    unto her anckle trailes:
Through which the shapes discerned bin,
    as too and fro it sailes.
Shapes both of men, who never lin
    to search her wonders out:
Of monsters and of Gods a kin,
    which her empale about.
A little world her flowing garment seemes:
And who but as a wonder thereof deemes?

For heere and there appeare forth towers,
    among the chalkie downes:
Citties among the Country bowers,
    which smiling Sun-shine crownes.
Her mettall buskins deckt with flowers,
    as th'earth when frosts are gone:
Besprinckled are with Orient showers
    of hayle and pebble stone.
Her feature peerelesse, peerelesse her attire,
I can but love her love, with zeale entire.

O who can sing her beauties best,
    or that remaines unsung?
Doe thou *Apollo* tune the rest,
    unworthy is my tongue.
To gaze on her, is to be blest,
    so wondrous fayre her face is;
Her fairenes cannot be exprest,
    in Goddesses nor Graces.
I love my love, the goodly worke of Nature:
Admire her face, but more admire her stature.

On thee (ô *Cosma*) will I gaze,
    and reade thy beauties ever:
Delighting in the blessed maze,
    which can be ended never.
For in the luster of thy rayes,
    appeares thy parents brightnes:
Who himselfe infinite displaies
    in thee his proper greatnes.
My song must end, but never my desire:
For *Cosmas* face is *Theorellos* fire.

                           E. B.

Sophi] also *Sophy, a wise man*   *Cauill,* probably *Caul*]
a covering of net-work   *nesh*] *soft*   *lin*] *cease*

Astrophels *Love is dead*

RING out your belles, let mourning shewes be spread,
    For Love is dead.
    All love is dead, infected
    With plague of deepe disdaine:
    Worth as nought worth rejected,
    And faith faire scorne doth gaine.
      From so ungratefull fancie,
      From such a femall frenzie,
      From them that use men thus:
       Good Lord deliver us.

Weepe neighbours weepe, doe you not heare it saide
    That Love is dead?
    His death-bed Peacocks follie,
    His winding sheete is shame:
    His will false, seeming holie,
    His sole exectour blame.
      From so ungratefull fancie,
      From such a female frenzie,
      From them that use men thus:
      Good Lord deliver us.

Let Dirge be sunge, and Trentals richly read,
    For Love is dead.
    And wrong his Tombe ordaineth,
    My Mistresse marble hart:
    Which Epitaph containeth,
    Her eyes were once his Dart.
      From so ungratefull fancie,
      From such a female frenzie,
      From them that use men thus:
      Good Lord deliver us.

Alas, I lye, rage hath this errour bred,
    Love is not dead.

Love is not dead, but sleepeth
In her unmatched minde:
Where shee his counsell keepeth,
Till due desert she find.
   Therefore from so vile fancie,
   To call such wit a frenzie,
   Who love can temper thus:
     Good Lord deliver us.

Sir Phil. Sidney

femall was a common spelling for *female*   *Trentals*] *a
set of thirty requiem masses*

A Palinode

As withereth the Primrose by the river,
As fadeth Sommers-sunne from gliding fountaines;
As vanisheth the light blowne bubble ever,
As melteth snow upon the mossie Mountaines.
So melts, so vanisheth, so fades, so withers,
The Rose, the shine, the bubble and the snow,
Of praise, pompe, glorie, joy (which short life
      gathers,)
Faire praise, vaine pompe, sweet glory, brittle joy.
The withered Primrose by the mourning river,
The faded Sommers-sunne from weeping fountaines:
The light-blowne bubble, vanished for ever,
The molten snow upon the naked mountaines,
    Are Emblems that the treasures we up-lay,
    Soone wither, vanish, fade, and melt away.

For as the snowe, whose lawne did over-spread
Th'ambitious hills, which Giant-like did threat
To pierce the heaven with theyr aspiring head,
Naked and bare doth leave their craggie seate.

8

When as the bubble, which did emptie flie
The daliance of the undiscerned winde:
On whose calme rowling waves it did relie,
Hath shipwrack made, where it did daliance finde:
And when the Sun-shine which dissolv'd the snow,
Cullourd the bubble with a pleasant varie,
And made the rathe and timely Primrose grow,
Swarth clowdes with-drawne (which longer time doe
      tarie)
    Oh what is praise, pompe, glory, joy, but so
    As shine by fountaines, bubbles, flowers or snow?

                                E. B.

rathe] *early*

Astrophell *the Sheep-heard, his complaint*
to his flocke

GOE my flocke, goe get yee hence,
    Seeke a better place of feeding:
Where yee may have some defence
    From the stormes in my breast breeding,
    And showers from mine eyes proceeding.

Leave a wretch, in whom all woe,
    can abide to keepe no measure:
Merry Flocke, such one forgoe
    unto whom mirth is displeasure,
    onely ritch in mischiefes treasure.

Yet (alas) before you goe,
    here your wofull Maisters Storie:
Which to stones I else would showe,
    Sorrow onely then hath glorie:
    when tis excellently sorrie.

Stella, fiercest Sheepheardesse,
    fiercest, but yet fairest ever:
Stella, whom the heavens still blesse,
    though against me she persever,
    though I blisse, inherite never.

Stella, hath refused me,
    Stella, who more love hath proved
In this caitiffe hart to be,
    Then can in good by us be moved:
    Towards Lambkins best beloved.

Stella, hath refused me,
    Astrophell that so well served,
In this pleasant Spring must see,
    while in pride flowers be preserved:
    himselfe onely Winter-sterved.

Why (alas) then dooth she sweare,
    that she loveth me so dearely:
Seeing me so long to beare
    coales of love that burne so clearly:
    and yet leave me helplesse meerely?

Is that love? Forsooth I trow,
    if I saw my good dogge greeved:
And a helpe for him did know,
    my Love should not be beleeved:
    but he were by me releeved.

No, she hates me, well away,
    faigning love, somewhat to please me:
Knowing, if she should display
    all her hate, Death soone would seaze me:
    and of hideous torments ease me.

Then my deare Flocke now adiew,
  but (alas) if in your straying,
Heavenly *Stella* meete with you,
  tell her in your pittious blaying:
  her poore slaves unjust decaying.

          S. Phil. Sidney

blaying] *bleating*

Hobbinolls *Dittie in prayse of* Eliza *Queene of the Sheepheards*

Yᴇᴇ dainty Nimphs that in this blessed Brooke
  Doo bath your brest;
Forsake your watry Bowers, and hether looke
  At my request.
And you faire Virgins that on *Parnasse* dwell,
Whence floweth *Helicon* the learned well:
   Helpe me to blaze
   Her worthy praise,
 Who in her sexe dooth all excell.

Of faire *Eliza* be your silver song,
  That blessed wight:
The flower of Virgins, may she flourish long,
  In Princely plight:
For shee is *Sirinx* daughter, without spot,
Which *Pan* the Sheepheards God on her begot:
   So sprung her Grace,
   Of heavenly race:
 No mortall blemish may her blot.

See where she sits upon the grassie greene,
  O seemely sight:
Yclad in scarlet, like a mayden Queene,
  And Ermines white.

11

Upon her head a crimson Coronet,
With Daffadills and Damaske Roses set,
Bay leaves betweene,
And Primeroses greene:
Embellish the sweet Violet.

Tell me, have ye beheld her Angels face,
Like *Phœbe* faire?
Her heavenly haviour, her Princely Grace,
Can well compare.
The red-Rose medled and the white yfere,
In eyther cheeke depeincten lively cheere.
Her modest eye,
Her Majestie,
Where have you seene the like but there?

I saw *Phœbus* thrust out his golden head,
On her to gaze:
But when he saw how broade her beames did
spread:
It did him maze.
He blusht to see an other Sunne below,
Ne durst againe his fierie face out-show:
Let him if he dare
His brightnes compare
With hers, to have the overthrow.

Shew thy selfe *Cinthia* with thy silver rayes,
And be not abasht,
When she the beames of her beauty displayes,
Oh how art thou dasht?
But I will not match her with *Latonaes* seede,
Such folly great sorrow to *Niobe* did breede,
Now is she a stone,
And makes deadly moane,
Warning all other to take heede.

Pan may be proud, that ever he begot
        Such a Bellibone:
And *Sirinx* rejoyce, that ever was her lot
        To beare such a one.
Soone as my Younglings cryen for the dam,
To her will I offer a milke-white Lamb.
        Shee is my Goddesse plaine,
        And I her Sheepheards Swaine,
Albe for-swonck and for-swat I am.

I see *Caliope* speede her to the place,
        Where my Goddesse shines:
And after her the other Muses trace
        With their Violines.
Bin they no Baie-braunches which they doo beare:
All for *Eliza* in her hand to weare?
        So sweetly they play,
        And sing all the way,
That it a heaven is to heare.

Loe how finely the *Graces* can it foote,
        to the Instrument:
They dauncen deffely and singen soote
        In their merriment.
Wants not a fourth *Grace* to make the daunce even?
Let that roome to my Lady be given.
        Shee shall be a *Grace*,
        To fill the fourth place,
And raigne with the rest in heaven.

And whether runnes this bevie of Ladies bright,
        Ranged in a roe?
They been all Ladies of the Lake behight
        That unto her goe:
Chloris, that is the chiefe Nimph of all,
Of Olive-braunches beares a Coronall:
        Olives beene for peace
        When warres doo surcease,
Such for a Princesse beene principall.

Bring hether the Pinke and purple Cullumbine.
>With Gillyflowers
Bring sweet Carnasions, and Sops in wine,
>Worne of Paramours.
Strew me the ground with Daffa-down-Dillies,
And Cowslips, and Kings-cups, and loved Lillies,
>The pretty Paunce,
>And the Chevisaunce,
>Shall match with the faire flower-Delice.

Ye Sheepheards daughters that dwell on the greene,
>Hie you there a pace,
Let none come there but such as Virgins beene,
>To adorne her Grace.
And when you come where as she is in place:
See that your rudenes doo not you disgrace.
>Bind your Fillets fast,
>And gird in your wast:
>For more finenesse with a Tawdrie lace.

Now rise up *Eliza*, decked as thou art,
>In royall ray:
And now ye dainty Damsels may depart,
>Each one her way.
I feare I have troubled your troupes too long:
Let dame *Eliza* thanke you for her Song.
>And if you come hether,
>When Damzins I gather
>I will part them all, you among.

>*Edm. Spencer*

yfere] together Bellibone, from *belle et bonne*] *a fair
lass   for-swonck and for-swat*] *out wearied and over
sweated   soote*] *sweetly   behight*] *called   sops in wine*]
some kind of carnation, no doubt mottled with red
Paunce] *pansy   chevisaunce*] possibly the wallflower
Tawdrie] *St. Awdrys'* lace, i.e. lace bought at St.

14

Awdry's fair. 'Gird in your waste' *E. H.* has 'on' but this is probably a misprint, 'in' is what Spenser wrote.

The Sheepheards Daffadill

GORBO, as thou cam'st this way
By yonder little hill,
Or as thou through the fields didst stray,
Saw'st thou my *Daffadill*?

Shee's in a frock of Lincolne greene,
The colour Maydes delight,
And never hath her Beauty seene
But through a vayle of white.

Then Roses richer to behold,
That dresse up Lovers Bowers,
The Pansie and the Marigold
Are *Phœbus* Paramoures.

Thou well describ'st the *Daffadill*,
It is not full an hower
Since by the Spring neere yonder hill
I saw that lovely flower.

Yet with my flower thou didst not meete,
Nor newes of her doest bring,
Yet is my *Daffadill* more sweete
Then that by yonder Spring.

I saw a Sheepheard that doth keepe
In yonder field of Lillies,
Was making (as he fed his sheepe)
A wreath of Daffadillies.

Yet *Gorbo:* thou delud'st me still,
My flower thou didst not see.
For know; my pretty *Daffadill*
Is worne of none but mee.

To shew it selfe but neere her seate
No Lilly is so bold,
Except to shade her from the heate,
Or keepe her from the cold.

Through yonder vale as I did passe
Descending from the hill,
I met a smerking Bonny-lasse,
They call her *Daffadill.*

Whose presence as a-long she went
The pretty flowers did greete,
As though their heads they downe-ward bent,
With homage to her feete.

And all the Sheepheards that were nie,
From top of every hill;
Unto the Vallies loud did crie,
There goes sweet *Daffadill.*

I gentle Sheepheard now with joy
Thou all my flock doest fill:
Come goe with me thou Sheepheards boy,
Let us to *Daffadill.*

Michaell Drayton

A Canzon Pastorall in honour of
her Majestie

ALAS what pleasure now the pleasant Spring
    Hath given place,
To harsh black frosts the sad ground covering,
    Can wee poore wee embrace,
When every bird on every branch can sing
    Naught but this note of woe alas?
Alas this note of woe why should we sound?
With us as May, September hath a prime,
Then birds and branches your alas is fond,
Which call upon the absent Sommer time:
      For did flowres make our May
      Or the Sun-beames your day,
When Night and Winter did the world embrace,
Well might you waile your ill and sing alas.

Loe Matron-like the Earth her selfe attires
    In habite grave,
Naked the fields are, bloomelesse are the brires,
    Yet we a Sommer have,
Who in our clime kindleth these living fires,
    Which bloomes can on the briers save.
No Ice dooth christallize the running Brooke,
No blast deflowres the flowre-adorned field,
Christall is cleere, but cleerer is the looke,
Which to our climes these living fires dooth yield:
      Winter though every where
      Hath no abiding heere:
On Brooks and Briers she doth rule alone,
The Sunne which lights our world is always one.

Edmund Bolton

fond] *foolish*

17

Melicertus *Madrigale*

WHAT are my Sheepe, without their wonted food?
What is my life, except I gaine my Love?
My Sheepe consume, and faint for want of blood,
My life is lost unlesse I *Grace* approve.
   No flower that saplesse thrives,
   No Turtle without pheare.

The day without the Sunne doth lower for woe
Then woe mine eyes, unlesse they beauty see:
My Sonne *Samelaes* eyes, by whom I know,
Wherein delight consists, where pleasures be.
   Nought more the hart revives,
   Then to embrace his Deare.

The starres from earthly humours gaine their light,
Our humours by their light possesse their power:
Samelaes eyes fed by my weeping sight,
Infuse my paines or joyes, by smile or lower.
   So wends the source of love,
   It feedes, it failes, it ends.

Kind lookes, cleare to your Joy, behold her eyes,
Admire her hart, desire to tast her kisses:
In them the heaven of joy and solace lyes,
Without them, every hope his succour misses.
   Oh how I live to proove,
   Whereto this solace tends?

        Ro. Greene

pheare] *companion*
live] love *Menaphon*

18

Olde Damons *Pastorall*

FROM Fortunes frownes and change remov'd,
    wend silly Flocks in blessed feeding:
None of *Damon* more belov'd,
    feede gentle Lambs while I sit reading.

Carelesse worldlings, outrage quelleth
    all the pride and pompe of Cittie:
But true peace with Sheepheards dwelleth,
    (Sheepheards who delight in pittie.)
Whether grace of heaven betideth,
    on our humble minds such pleasure:
Perfect peace with Swaines abideth,
    love and faith is Sheepheards treasure.
On the lower Plaines the thunder
    little thrives, and nought prevaileth:
Yet in Citties breedeth wonder,
    and the highest hills assaileth.

Envie of a forraigne Tyrant
    threatneth Kings, not Sheepheards humble:
Age makes silly Swaines delirant,
    thirst of rule garres great men stumble.
What to other seemeth sorrie,
    abject state and humble biding:
Is our joy and Country glorie,
    highest states have worse betiding.
Golden cups doo harbour poyson,
    and the greatest pompe, dissembling:
Court of seasoned words hath foyson,
    treason haunts in most assembling.

Homely breasts doo harbour quiet,
    little feare, and mickle solace:
States suspect their bed and diet,
    feare and craft doo haunt the Pallace.

Little would I, little want I,
    where the mind and store agreeth,
Smallest comfort is not scantie,
    least he longs that little seeth.
Time hath beene that I have longed,
    foolish I, to like of follie:
To converse where honour thronged,
    to my pleasures linked wholy.

Now I see, and seeing sorrow
    that the day consum'd, returnes not:
Who dare trust upon to morrow,
    when nor time, not life sojournes not?

Thom. Lodge

delirant] raving   garres] makes   foyson] plenty

Perigot *and* Cuddies *Roundelay*

It fell upon a holy-Eve,
    hey hoe holy-day:
When holy-Fathers wont to shrive,
    now ginneth this Roundelay.
Sitting upon a hill so hie,
    hey hoe the hie hill:
The while my flocke did feede thereby,
    the while the Sheepheards selfe did spill.

I saw the bouncing Bellybone,
    hey hoe Bonny-bell:
Tripping over the Dale alone,
    shee can trip it very well.
Well decked in a Frock of gray,
    hey hoe gray is greete:
And in a Kirtle of greene Say,
    the greene is for Maydens meete.

20

A Chaplet on her head she wore,
　　hey hoe the Chaplet:
Of sweet Violets therein was store,
　　she's sweeter then the Violet.
My Sheepe did leave their wonted food,
　　hey hoe silly Sheepe:
And gaz'd on her as they were wood,
　　wood as he that did them keepe.

As the Bony-lasse passed by,
　　hey hoe Bony-lasse:
Shee rold at me with glauncing eye,
　　as cleare as the Christall-glasse.
All as the Sunnie-beame so bright,
　　hey hoe the Sun-beame:
Glaunceth from *Phœbus* face forth right,
　　so love into my heart did streame.

Or as the thunder cleaves the clouds,
　　hey hoe the thunder:
Wherein the lightsome levin shrouds,
　　so cleaves my soule a-sunder.
Or as Dame *Cinthias* silver ray,
　　hey hoe the moone-light:
Upon the glistering wave doth play,
　　such play is a pitteous plight.

The glaunce into my hart did glide,
　　hey hoe the glider:
There-with my soule was sharply gride,
　　such wounds soone wexen wider.
Hasting to raunch the arrow out,
　　hey hoe *Perigot:*
I left the head in my hart roote,
　　it was a desperate shot.

21

There it rankleth aye more and more,
 hey hoe the arrow:
Ne can I finde salue for my sore,
 love is a curelesse sorrow.
And though my bale with death I bought,
 hey hoe heavie cheere:
Yet should thilke lasse not from my thought,
 so you may buy gold too deere.

But whether in painfull love I pine,
 hey hoe pinching paine:
Or thrive in wealth, she shall be mine,
 but if thou can her obtaine.
And if for gracelesse greefe I dye
 hey hoe gracelesse greefe:
Witnesse, she slew me with her eye,
 let thy folly be the preefe.

And you that saw it, simple sheepe.
 hey hoe the faire flocke:
For priefe thereof my death shall weepe,
 and moane with many a mocke.
So learn'd I love on a holy-Eve,
 hey hoe holy-day:
That ever since my hart did greeve,
 now endeth our Roundelay.

       Edm. Spencer

greete] obsolete form of *great*   *Say*] probably a
mixture of silk and wool
wood] *distracted*   *levin*] *lightning*   *gride*] *pierced*
bale] *sorrow*   *preefe, priefe*] *proof*

Phillida *and* Coridon

In the merry moneth of May,
In a morne by breake of day,
Foorth I walked by the Wood side,
When as May was in his pride:
There I spied all alone,
Phillida and *Coridon*.
Much a-doo there was God wot,
He would love, and she would not.
She sayd never man was true,
He sayd, none was false to you.
He sayd, he had loved her long,
She sayd, Love should have no wrong.
Coridon would kisse her then,
She said, Maides must kisse no men,
Till they did for good and all.
Then she made the Sheepheard call
All the heavens to witnesse truth:
Never lov'd a truer youth.
Thus with many a pretty oath,
Yea and nay, and faith and troth,
Such as silly Sheepheards use,
When they will not Love abuse;
Love, which had beene long deluded,
Was with kisses sweete concluded.
And *Phillida* with garlands gay:
Was made the Lady of the May.

N. Breton

To Colin Cloute

BEAUTIE sate bathing by a Spring,
    where fayrest shades did hide her.
The winds blew calme, the birds did sing,
    the coole streames ranne beside her.
My wanton thoughts entic'd mine eye,
    to see what was forbidden:
But better Memory said, fie,
    so, vaine Desire was chidden.
    hey nonnie, nonnie, &c.

Into a slumber then I fell,
    when fond imagination:
Seemed to see, but could not tell
    her feature or her fashion.
But even as Babes in dreames doo smile,
    and sometime fall a weeping:
So I awakt, as wise this while,
    as when I fell a sleeping.
    hey nonnie, nonnie, &c.

Sheepheard Tonie

Rowlands *Song in praise of the fairest* Beta

O THOU silver Thames, ô clearest christall flood,
Beta alone the Phœnix is of all thy watry brood.
The Queene of Virgins only she,
And thou the Queene of floods shalt be.
Let all the Nimphs be jcyfull then, to see this happy
    day:
Thy *Beta* now alone shall be the subject of my Lay.

With dainty and delightsome straines of sweetest
    Virelayes,
Come lovely Sheepheards sit we down, & chaunt our
    Betas praise.
And let us sing so rare a verse,
Our *Betas* praises to rehearse:
That little birds shall silent be, to heare poore Sheep-
    heards sing:
And Rivers backward bend their course, & flow unto
    the spring.

Range all thy Swannes faire Thames together on a
    ranke:
And place them duly one by one upon thy stately
    banke.
Then set together all a-good,
Recording to the silver flood:
And crave the tunefull Nightingale to helpe ye with
    her Lay:
The Osell and the Thrustlecocke, chiefe musique of
    our May.

O see what troupes of Nimphs been sporting on the
    strands,
And they been blessed Nimphs of peace, with Olives
    in their hands.
How merrily the Muses sing,
That all the flowrie meddowes ring,
And *Beta* sits upon the banke in purple and in pall,
And she the Queene of Muses is, and weares the
    Coronall.

Trim up her golden tresses with *Apollos* sacred tree,
O happy sight unto all those that love and honour
    thee,
The blessed Angels have prepar'd
A glorious crowne for thy reward,
Not such a golden crowne as haughty *Cæsar* weares:
But such a glittering starrie crowne as *Ariadne* beares.

Make her a goodly Chaplet of azurd Cullumbine,
And wreath about her Coronet with sweetest
    Eglantine.
Bedeck our *Beta* all with Lillies
And the dainty Daffadillies,
With Roses Damaske, white and red, and fairest
    flowre-Delice:
With Cowslips of Jerusalem, and Cloaves of
    Paradice.

O thou faire Torch of heaven, the days most dearest
    light,
And thou bright-shining *Cinthia*, the glory of the
    night.
You starres the eyes of heaven,
And thou the glyding leven,
And thou ô gorgeous *Iris*, with all strange colours
    dyed:
When she streames foorth her rayes, then dasht is all
    your pride.

See how the Day stands still, admiring of her face,
And Time loe stretcheth foorth his armes thy *Beta* to
    embrace.
The Sirens sing sweete Layes,
The Trytons sound her prayse,
Goe passe on Thames, and hie thee fast unto the
    Ocean Sea:
And let thy billowes there proclaime thy *Betas* holy-
    day.

And water thou the blessed roote of that greene Olive
    tree,
With whose sweete shadow all thy bancks with peace
    preserved be.
Laurell for Poets and Conquerours:
And Mirtle for Loves Paramours.

That fame may be thy fruite, the boughs preserved by
    peace,
And let the mournfull Cypres die, now stormes and
    tempests cease.

Weele strew the shoare with pearle, where *Beta* walks
    a-lone,
And we will pave her Princely Bower with richest
    Indian stone.
Perfume the ayre, and make it sweete,
For such a Goddesse it is meete.
For if her eyes for purity contend with *Titans* light:
No mervaile then, although they so doo dazell
    humaine sight.

Sound out your Trumpets then from Londons stately
    Towers,
To beate the stormie winds a-backe, and calme the
    raging showers.
Set to the Cornet and the Flute,
The Orpharion and the Lute:
And tune the Taber and the Pipe to the sweet
    Violons:
And moove the thunder in the ayre with lowdest
    Clarions.

Beta, long may thine Altars smoake with yeerely
    sacrifise,
And long thy sacred temples may their Sabaoths
    solemnise.
Thy Sheepheards watch by day and night,
Thy Maides attend the holy light,
And thy large Empire stretch her armes from East
    unto the West:
And *Albion* on the *Appenines* advaunce her
    conquering crest.

                     Mich. Drayton

Virelayes] *a song or short lyric piece*   *Orpharion*] *a
large kind of lute*

27

The Barginet of Antimachus

In pride of youth, in midst of May,
When birds with many a merry Lay,
        salute the Sunnes up-rising:
I sate me downe fast by a Spring,
And while these merry Chaunters sing,
        I fell upon surmizing.
Amidst my doubt and minds debate,
Of change of time, of worlds estate,
        I spyed a boy attired
In silver plumes, yet naked quite,
Save pretty feathers fit for flight,
        wherewith he still aspired.
A bowe he bare to worke mens wrack,
A little Quiver at his back,
        with many arrowes filled:
And in his soft and pretty hand,
He held a lively burning brand,
        where-with he Lovers killed.
Fast by his side, in rich aray,
There sate a lovely Lady gay,
        his mother as I guessed:
That set the Lad upon her knee,
And trimd his bowe, and taught him flee,
        And mickle Love professed.
Oft from her lap at sundry stoures,
He leapt, and gathered Sommer flowres,
        both Violets and Roses:
But see the chaunce that followed fast,
As he the pompe of prime dooth wast,
        before that he supposes:
A Bee that harbour'd hard thereby,
Did sting his hand, and made him crye
        Oh Mother, I am wounded:
Faire *Venus* that beheld her Sonne,
Cryed out alas, I am undone,
        and there-upon she swounded.

My little Lad the Goddesse sayd,
Who hath my *Cupid* so dismayd?
   he aunswered: Gentle Mother
The hony-worker in the Hive,
My greefe and mischiefe dooth contrive,
   alas it is none other.
Shee kist the Lad: Now marke the chaunce,
And straite she fell into a traunce,
   and crying, thus concluded:
Ah wanton boy, like to the Bee,
Thou with a kisse hast wounded me,
   and haplesse Love included.
A little Bee dooth thee affright,
But ah, my wounds are full of spright,
   and cannot be recured:
The boy that kist his Mothers paine,
Gan smile, and kist her whole againe,
   and made her hope assured.
She suckt the wound, and swag'd the sting,
And little Love ycurde did sing,
   then let no Lover sorrow:
To day though greefe attaint his hart,
Let him with courage bide the smart,
   amends will come to morrow.

        Thom. Lodge

Barginet] *a rustic dance, accompanied by a song*
stoures] probably the word here means *occasions*
swag'd] *assuaged*

Menaphons *Roundelay*

WHEN tender Ewes brought home with evenings
    Sun,
Wend to their Folds,
And to their holds
The Sheepheards trudge when light of day is done:
Upon a tree,
The Eagle *Joves* faire bird did pearch,
There resteth hee.
A little Flie his harbour then did search,
And did presume, (though others laugh'd thereat)
To pearch whereas the Princely Eagle sat.

The Eagle frownd, and shooke his royall wings,
And charg'd the Flie
From thence to hie.
Afraide, in haste the little creature flings,
Yet seekes againe,
Fearefull to pearke him by the Eagles side.
With moodie vaine
The speedie poast of *Ganimede* replide:
Vassaile avaunt, or with my wings you die.
Is't fit an Eagle seate him with a Flie?

The Flie crav'd pitty, still the Eagle frownd.
The silly Flie
Ready to die:
Disgrac'd, displac'd, fell groveling to the ground.
The Eagle sawe:
And with a royall mind said to the Flie,
Be not in awe,
I scorne by me the meanest creature die.
Then seate thee heere: The joyfull Flie up-flings,
And sate safe shadowed with the Eagles wings.

Ro. Greene

pearke] obsolete form of *pearch*

A Pastorall of Phillis and Coridon

On a hill there growes a flower,
    faire befall the dainty sweete:
By that flower there is a Bower,
    where the heavenly Muses meete.

In that Bower there is a chaire,
    frindged all about with gold:
Where dooth sit the fairest faire,
    that ever eye did yet behold.

It is *Phillis* faire and bright,
    shee that is the Sheepheards joy:
Shee that *Venus* did despight,
    and did blind her little boy.

This is she, the wise, the rich,
    That the world desires to see:
This is *ipsa quæ* the which,
    there is none but onely shee.

Who would not this face admire?
    who would not this Saint adore?
Who would not this sight desire,
    though he thought to see no more?

Oh faire eyes, yet let me see,
    for one good looke, and I am gone:
Looke on me, for I am hee,
    thy poore silly *Coridon*.

Thou that art the Sheepheards Queene,
    looke upon thy silly Swaine:
By thy comfort have beene seene
    dead men brought to life againe.

N. Breton

Coridon *and* Melampus *Song*

Cor. MELAMPUS, when will Love be void of feares?
Mel. When Jealousie hath neither eyes nor eares.
Cor. Melampus, when will Love be throughly
      shrieved?
Mel. When it is hard to speake, and not beleeved.
Cor. Melampus, when is Love most malecontent?
Mel. When Lovers range, and beare their bowes un-
      bent.
Cor. Melampus, tell me, when takes Love least
      harme?
Mel. When Swaines sweet pipes are puft, and Trulls
      are warme.
Cor. Melampus, tell me, when is Love best fed?
Mel. When it hath suck'd the sweet that ease hath
      bred.
Cor. Melampus, when is time in Love ill spent?
Mel. When it earnes meede, and yet receaves no
      rent.
Cor. Melampus, when is time well spent in Love?
Mel. When deedes win meedes, and words Loves
      works doo prove.

                   Geo. Peele

Trulls] lasses

Tityrus *to his faire* Phillis

THE silly Swaine whose love breedes discontent,
Thinks death a trifle, life a loathsome thing,
        Sad he lookes, sad he lyes:
But when his Fortunes mallice dooth relent,
Then of Loves sweetnes he will sweetly sing,
        thus he lives, thus he dyes.

Then *Tityrus* whom Love hath happy made,
Will rest thrice happy in this Mirtle shade.
                    For though Love at first did
                         greeve him:
                    yet did Love at last releeve him.

                                        J. D.

Sheepheard

SWEETE thrall, first step to Loves felicitie,
                    Sheepheardesse.
Sweete thrall, no stop to perfect libertie.
          Hee. O Life. *Shee.* What life?
          Hee. Sweete life. *Shee.* No life more
               sweete:
          Hee. O Love. *Shee.* What love?
          Hee. Sweete Love. *Shee.* No love more
               meete.

                                        J. M.

Another of the same Authour

FIELDS were over-spread with flowers,
Fairest choise of *Floraes* treasure:
Sheepheards there had shadie Bowers,
Where they oft reposed with pleasure.
                    Meadowes flourish'd fresh and gay,
                    where the wanton Heards did play.

Springs more cleare then Christall streames,
Seated were the Groves among:
Thus nor *Titans* scorching beames,
Nor earths drouth could Sheepheards wrong.
   Faire *Pomonaes* fruitfull pride:
   did the budding braunches hide.

Flocks of sheepe fed on the Plaines,
Harmelesse sheepe that roamd at large:
Heere and there sate pensive Swaines,
Wayting on their wandring charge.
   Pensive while their Lasses smil'd:
   Lasses which had them beguil'd.

Hills with trees were richly dight,
Vallies stor'd with *Vestaes* wealth:
Both did harbour sweet delight,
Nought was there to hinder health.
   Thus did heaven grace the soyle:
   Not deform'd with work-mens toile.

Purest plot of earthly mold,
Might that Land be justly named:
Art by Nature was controld,
Art which no such pleasures framed.
   Fayrer place was never seene:
   Fittest place for Beauties Queene.

            J. M.

dight] *clothed*

Menaphon *to* Pesana

FAIRE fields proud *Floraes* vaunt, why i'st you smile,
        when as I languish?
You golden Meades, why strive you to beguile
        my weeping anguish?
I live to sorrow, you to pleasure spring,
        why doo ye spring thus?
What, will not *Boreas* tempests wrathfull King,
        take some pitty on us?
And send forth Winter in her rustie weede,
        to waile my bemoanings:
While I distrest doo tune my Country Reede
        unto my groanings.
But heaven and earth, time, place, and every power,
        have with her conspired:
To turne my blisfull sweete to balefull sower,
        since I fond desired
The heaven whereto my thoughts may not aspire,
        aye me unhappie:
It was my fault t'imbrace my bane the fire
        that forceth me die.
Mine be the paine, but hers the cruell cause,
        of this strange torment:
Wherefore no time my banning prayers shall pause,
        till proud she repent.

Ro. Greene

A sweete Pastorall

GOOD Muse rock me a sleepe,
        with some sweet Harmonie:
This wearie eye is not to keepe
        thy warie companie.

Sweete Love be gone a while,
        thou knowest my heavines:
Beauty is borne but to beguile,
        my hart of happines.

See how my little flocke
        that lov'd to feede on hie:
Doo headlong tumble downe the Rocke,
        and in the Vallie die.

The bushes and the trees
        that were so fresh and greene:
Doo all their dainty colour leese,
        and not a leafe is seene.

The Black-bird and the Thrush,
        that made the woods to ring:
With all the rest, are now at hush,
        and not a noate they sing.

Sweete *Philomele* the bird,
        that hath the heavenly throate,
Dooth now alas not once affoord
        recording of a noate.

The flowers have had a frost,
        each hearbe hath lost her savour:
And *Phillida* the faire hath lost,
        the comfort of her favour.

Now all these careful sights,
        so kill me in conceite:
That how to hope upon delights
        it is but meere deceite.

And therefore my sweete Muse
        that knowest what helpe is best,
Doo now thy heavenly cunning use,
        to set my hart at rest.

And in a dreame bewray
      what fate shall be my friend:
Whether my life shall still decay,
      or when my sorrow end.

N. Breton

leese] *lose*

Harpalus *complaynt on* Phillidaes *love bestowed on* Corin, *who loved her not, and denyed him that loved her*

PHILLIDA was a faire mayde,
    as fresh as any flower:
Whom *Harpalus* the Heards-man prayde
    to be his Paramour.
Harpalus and eke *Corin*,
    were Heard-men both yfere:
And *Phillida* could twist and spinne,
    and thereto sing full cleere.
But *Phillida* was all too coy,
    for *Harpalus* to winne:
For *Corin* was her onely joy,
    who forc'd her not a pinne.
How often would she flowers twine,
    how often garlands make:
Of Cowslips and of Cullumbine,
    and all for *Corins* sake?
But *Corin* he had Hawkes to lure,
    and forced more the field:
Of Lovers law he tooke no cure,
    for once he was beguild.
Harpalus prevailed naught,
    his labour all was lost:

For he was furthest from her thought,
    and yet he lov'd her most.
Therefore woxe he both pale and leane,
    and drye as clod of clay:
His flesh it was consumed cleane,
    his colour gone away.
His beard it had not long beene shaue,
    his haire hung all unkempt:
A man most fit even for the grave,
    whom spitefull Love had spent.
His eyes were red and all fore-watcht,
    his face besprent with teares:
It seem'd unhap had him long hatcht,
    in midst of his dispaires.
His cloathes were blacke and also bare,
    as one forlorne was hee:
Upon his head he always ware
    a wreath of Willow-tree.
His beasts he kept upon the hill,
    and he sate in the Dale:
And thus with sighs and sorrowes shrill,
    he gan to tell his tale.
Oh *Harpalus*, thus would he say,
    unhappiest under Sunne:
The cause of thine unhappy day,
    by love was first begun.
For thou went'st first by sute to seeke,
    a Tyger to make tame:
That sets not by thy love a Leeke,
    but makes thy greefe a game.
As easie were it to convert
    the frost into a flame:
As for to turne a froward hart
    whom thou so faine wouldst frame.
Corin, he liveth carelesse,
    he leapes among the leaves:
He eates the fruites of thy redresse,
    thou reap'st, he takes the sheaves.

My beasts a-while your food refraine,
 and harke your Heard-mans sound:
Whom spightfull Love alas hath slaine,
 through-girt with many a wound.
Oh happy be ye beasts wild,
 that heere your pasture takes:
I see that ye be not beguild,
 of these your faithfull makes.
The Hart he feedeth by the Hind,
 the Bucke hard by the Doe:
The Turtle-Dove is not unkind
 to him that loves her so.
The Ewe she hath by her the Ram,
 the young Cowe hath the Bull:
The Calfe with many a lusty Lamb,
 doo feede their hunger full.
But well-away that Nature wrought,
 thee *Phillida* so faire:
For I may say that I have bought
 thy beauty all too deare.
What reason is't that cruelty
 with beauty should have part?
Or else that such great tirannie,
 should dwell in womans hart?
I see therefore to shape my death,
 she cruelly is prest:
To th'end that I may want my breath,
 my dayes beene at the best.
Oh *Cupid* graunt this my request,
 and doo not stop thine eares:
That she may feele within her brest,
 the paine of my despaires.
Of *Corin* that is carelesse,
 that she may crave her fee:
As I have done in great distresse,
 that lov'd her faithfully.
But since that I shall die her slave,
 her slave and eke her thrall:

Write you my friends upon my grave,
    this chaunce that is befall.
Heere lyeth unhappy *Harpalus*,
    by cruell Love now slaine:
Whom *Phillida* unjustly thus,
    hath murdred with disdaine.

yfere] together spent] exhausted hatcht] marked with
lines makes] companions

            L. T. Haward, Earle of Surrie

Another of the same subject, but made as it were in aunswere

ON a goodly Sommers day,
Harpalus and *Phillida*,
He a true harted Swaine,
Shee full of coy disdaine,
        drove their flocks to field:
He to see his Sheepheardesse,
She did dreame on nothing lesse,
Than his continuall care,
Which to grim-fac'd Dispaire,
        wholely did him yield.
Corin she affected still,
All the more thy hart to kill.
Thy case dooth make me rue,
That thou should'st love so true,
        and be thus disdain'd:
While their flocks a feeding were,
They did meete together there.
Then with a curtsie lowe,
And sighs that told his woe,
        thus to her he plain'd.

Bide a while faire *Phillida*,
List what *Harpalus* will say
Onely in love to thee,
Though thou respect not mee,
        yet vouchsafe an eare:
To prevent ensuing ill,
Which no doubt betide thee will,
If thou doo not fore-see,
To shunne it presentlie,
        then thy harme I feare.
Firme thy love is, well I wot,
To the man that loves thee not.
Lovely and gentle mayde,
Thy hope is quite betrayde,
        which my hart doth greeve:
Corin is unkind to thee,
Though thou thinke contrarie.
His love is growne as light,
As is his Faulcons flight,
        this sweet Nimph beleeve.

Mopsus daughter, that young mayde,
Her bright eyes his hart hath strayde
From his affecting thee,
Now there is none but shee
        That is *Corins* blisse:
Phillis men the Virgin call,
She is Buxome, faire and tall,
Yet not like *Phillida*:
If I my mind might say,
        eyes oft deeme amisse.
He commends her beauty rare,
Which with thine may not compare.
He dooth extoll her eye,
Silly thing, if thine were by,
        thus conceite can erre:

He is ravish'd with her breath,
Thine can quicken life in death.
He prayseth all her parts,
Thine, winnes a world of harts,
         more, if more there were.

Looke sweet Nimph upon thy flock,
They stand still, and now feede not,
As if they shar'd with thee:
Greefe for this injurie,
         offred to true love.
Pretty Lambkins, how they moane,
And in bleating seeme to groane,
That any Sheepheards Swaine,
Should cause their Mistres paine:
         by affects remove.
If you looke but on the grasse,
It's not halfe so greene as 'twas:
When I began my tale,
But is as witherd pale,
         all in meere remorce.
Marke the Trees that brag'd even now,
Of each goodly greene-leav'd-bow,
They seeme as blasted all,
Ready for Winters fall,
         such is true loves force.

The gentle murmur of the Springs,
Are become contrary things,
They have forgot their pride,
And quite forsake their glide,
         as if charm'd they stand.
And the flowers growing by,
Late so fresh in every eye,
See how they hang the head,
As on a suddaine dead,
         dropping on the sand.

The birds that chaunted it yer-while,
Ere they hear'd of *Corins* guile,
Sit as they were afraide,
Or by some hap dismaide,
    for this wrong to thee:
Harke sweet *Phil*, how *Philomell*,
That was wont to sing so well,
Jargles now in yonder bush,
Worser than the rudest Thrush,
    as it were not shee.

Phillida, who all this while
Neither gave a sigh or smile:
Round about the field did gaze,
As her wits were in a maze,
    poore despised mayd.
And revived at the last,
After streames of teares were past,
Leaning on her Sheepheards hooke,
With a sad and heavie looke,
    thus poore soule she sayd.
Harpalus, I thanke not thee,
For this sorry tale to mee.
Meete me heere againe to morrow,
Then I will conclude my sorrow
    mildly, if may be:
With their flocks they home doo fare,
Eythers hart too full of care,
If they doo meete againe,
Then what they furder sayne,
    you shall heare from me.

       Shep. Tonie

The Nimphes meeting their May Queene, entertaine her with this Dittie

WITH fragrant flowers we strew the way,
And make this our cheefe holy-day.
For though this clime were blest of yore:
Yet was it never proud before.
   O beauteous Queene of second Troy:
   Accept of our unfayned joy.

Now th' Ayre is sweeter than sweet Balme,
And Satires daunce about the Palme,
Now earth with verdure newly dight,
Gives perfect signes of her delight.
   O beauteous Queene, &c.

Now birds record new harmonie,
And trees doo whistle melodie,
Now every thing that Nature breedes,
Dooth clad it selfe in pleasant weedes.
   O beauteous Queene, &c.

       Tho. Watson

proud] this may be *provd = prov'd*, see p. xxi
dight] *clothed* or *covered*

Colin Cloutes *mournfull Dittie for the death of* Astrophell

SHEEPHEARDS that wunt on pipes of Oaten reede,
Oft-times to plaine your loves concealed smart;
And with your pitteous Layes have learn'd to breede
Compassion in a Country-Lasses hart:

44

Harken ye gentle Sheepheards to my song,
And place my dolefull plaint your plaints among.

To you alone I sing this mournful verse,
The mournfulst verse that ever man heard tell:
To you whose softned harts it may empierse
With dolours dart for death of *Astrophell*.
To you I sing, and to none other wight:
For well I wot, my rimes been rudely dight.

Yet as they been, if any nicer wit
Shall hap to heare, or covet them to reade:
Thinke he, that such are for such ones most fit,
Made not to please the living, but the dead.
And if in him found pitty ever place:
Let him be moov'd to pitty such a case.

Edm. Spencer

dight] *composed*

Damætas *Jigge in praise of his Love*

JOLLY Sheepheard, Sheepheard on a hill
        on a hill so merrily,
        on a hill so cherily,
Feare not Sheepheard there to pipe thy fill,
Fill every Dale, fill every Plaine:
        both sing and say; Love feeles no paine.

Jolly Sheepheard, Sheepheard on a greene
        on a greene so merrily,
        on a greene so cherily,
Be thy voyce shrill, be thy mirth seene,
Heard to each Swaine, seene to each Trull:
        both sing and say; Loves joy is full.

Jolly Sheepheard, Sheepheard in the Sunne,
       in the Sunne so merrily,
       in the Sunne so cherily,
Sing forth thy songs, and let thy rimes runne
Downe to the Dales, to the hills above:
       both sing and say; No life to love.

Jolly Sheepheard, Sheepheard in the shade,
       in the shade so merrily,
       in the shade so cherily,
Joy in thy life, life of Sheepheards trade,
Joy in thy love, love full of glee:
       both sing and say; Sweet Love for me.

Jolly Sheepheard, Sheepheard heere or there,
       heere or there so merrily,
       heere or there so cherily,
Or in thy chat, eyther at thy cheere,
In every Jigge, in every Lay:
       both sing and say; Love lasts for aye.

Jolly Sheepheard, Sheepheard, *Daphnis* Love,
       Daphnis love so merrily,
       Daphnis love so cherily,
Let thy fancie never more remove,
Fancie be fixt, fixt not to fleete,
       still sing and say; Loves yoake is sweete.

                      John Wootton

Montanus *praise of his faire* Phæbe

PHÆBE sate
Sweete she sate,
       sweet sate *Phœbe* when I saw her,

White her brow
Coy her eye,
>   brow and eye, how much you please me?

Words I spent,
Sighs I sent,
>   sighs and words could never draw her,

Oh my Love,
Thou art lost,
>   since no sight could ever ease thee.

Phœbe sate
By a Fount,
>   sitting by a Fount I spide her,

Sweete her touch,
Rare her voyce,
>   touch and voyce, what may distaine you?

As she sung,
I did sigh,
>   And by sighs whilst that I tride her,

Oh mine eyes
You did loose,
>   her first sight whose want did paine you.

Phœbes flocks
White as wooll,
>   yet were *Phœbes* lookes more whiter,

Phœbes eyes
Dove-like mild,
>   Dove-like eyes both mild and cruell,

Montane sweares
In your Lamps,
>   he will die for to delight her,

Phœbe yeeld
Or I die,
>   shall true harts be fancies fuell?

>   *Thom. Lodge*

distaine] *to dim or outshine*

47

The complaint of Thestilis the forsaken Sheepheard

THESTILIS a silly Swaine, when Love did him forsake,
In mournfull wise amid the woods, thus gan his plaint
    to make.
Ah wofull man (quoth he) falne is thy lot to mone,
And pine away with carefull thoughts, unto thy Love
    unknowne.
Thy Nimph forsakes thee quite, whom thou didst
    honour so:
That aye to her thou wert a friend, but to thyselfe a
    foe.
Ye Lovers that have lost your harts-desired choyce:
Lament with me my cruell hap, and helpe my tremb-
    ling voyce.
Was never man that stoode so great in Fortunes grace,
Nor with his sweate (alas too deere) possest so high a
    place:
As I whose simple hart, aye thought himselfe still sure,
But now I see high springing tides, they may not aye
    endure.
Shee knowes my guiltlesse hart, and yet she lets it pine:
Of her untrue professed love, so feeble is the twine.
What wonder is it then, if I berent my haires:
And craving death continually, doo bathe my selfe in
    teares?
When *Cræsus* King of *Lide*, was cast in cruell bands,
And yeelded goods and life into his enemies hands:
What tongue could tell his woe? yet was his griefe
    much lesse
Then mine, for I have lost my Love, which might my
    woe redresse.
Ye woods that shroud my limbs, give now your hollow
    sound:
That ye may helpe me to bewaile, the cares that me
    confound.

Ye Rivers rest a while, and stay your streames that
     runne:
Rue *Thestilis*, the wofulst man that rests under the
     Sunne.
Transport my sighs ye winds, unto my pleasant foe:
My trickling teares shall witnes beare, of this my cruell
     woe.
Oh happy man were I, if all the Gods agreed:
That now the Sisters three should cut in twaine my
     fatall threed.
Till life with love shall end, I heere resigne all joy,
Thy pleasant sweete I now lament, whose lacke breeds
     mine annoy.
Farewell my deere therefore, farewell to me well
     knowne,
If that I die, it shall be sayd: that thou hast slaine thine
     owne.

                                   L. T. Howard, E. of Surrie

berent] tear

To Phillis *the faire Sheepheardesse*

My *Phillis* hath the morning Sunne,
     at first to looke upon her:
And *Phillis* hath morne-waking birds,
     her risings still to honour.
My *Phillis* hath prime-feathered flowres,
     that smile when she treads on them:
And *Phillis* hath a gallant flocke,
     that leapes since she dooth owne them.
But *Phillis* hath too hard a hart,
     alas that she should have it:
It yeelds no mercie to desert,
          nor grace to those that crave it.

Sweete Sunne, when thou look'st on,
           pray her regard my moane.
Sweete birds, when you sing to her,
           to yeeld some pitty, woo her.
Sweete flowers that she treads on,
           tell her, her beauty deads one.
  And if in life her love she nill agree me:
  Pray her before I die, she will come see me.

S. E. D.

nill] *will not*

The Sheepheard Dorons *Jigge*

THROUGH the shrubs as I can crack,
       for my Lambs pretty ones,
       mongst many little ones,
Nimphs I meane, whose haire was black
            As the Crow.
            Like as the Snow
Her face and browes shin'd I weene,
       I saw a little one,
       a bonny pretty one,
As bright, buxome, and as sheene:
            As was shee
            On her knee
That lull'd the God, whose arrowes warmes
       such merry little ones,
       such faire-fac'd pretty ones,
As dally in Loves chiefest harmes.
            Such was mine,
            Whose gray eyne
Made me love: I gan to wooe
       this sweete little one,
       this bonny pretty one.

I wooed hard a day or two,
>> Till she bad,
>> Be not sad,
Wooe no more, I am thine owne,
> thy dearest little one,
> thy truest pretty one.
Thus was faith and firme love showne,
>> As behooves
>> Sheepheards Loves.

Ro. Greene

can] did   sheene] *fair, beautiful*

Astrophell *his Song of* Phillida *and* Coridon

FAIRE in a morne, (ô fairest morne)
> was never morne so faire:
There shone a Sunne, though not the Sunne,
> that shineth in the ayre.
For the earth, and from the earth,
> (was never such a creature:)
Did come this face, (was never face,)
> that carried such a feature.
Upon a hill, (ô blessed hill,
> was never hill so blessed)
There stoode a man, (was never man
> for woman so distressed.)
This man beheld a heavenly view,
> which did such vertue give:
As cleares the blind, and helps the lame,
> and makes the dead man live.
This man had hap, (ô happy man
> more happy none then hee;)
For he had hap to see the hap,
> that none had hap to see.

51

This silly Swaine, (and silly Swaines
        are men of meanest grace:)
Had yet the grace, (ô gracious guest)
        to hap on such a face.
He pitty cryed, and pitty came,
        and pittied so his paine:
As dying, would not let him die,
        but gave him life againe.
For joy whereof he made such mirth,
        as all the woods did ring:
And *Pan* with all his Swaines came foorth,
        to heare the Sheepheard sing.
But such a Song sung never was,
        nor shall be sung againe:
Of *Phillida* the Sheepheards Queene,
        and *Coridon* the Swaine.
Faire *Phillis* is the Sheepheards Queene,
        (was never such a Queene as she,)
And *Coridon* her onely Swaine,
        (was never such a Swaine as he.)
Faire *Phillis* hath the fairest face,
        that ever eye did yet behold:
And *Coridon* the constants faith,
        that ever yet kept flocke in fold.
Sweete *Phillis* is the sweetest sweete,
        that ever yet the earth did yeeld:
And *Coridon* the kindest Swaine,
        that ever yet kept Lambs in field.
Sweete *Philomell* is *Phillis* bird,
        though *Coridon* be he that caught her:
And *Coridon* dooth heare her sing,
        though *Phillida* be she that taught her.
Poore *Coridon* dooth keepe the fields,
        though *Phillida* be she that owes them:
And *Phillida* dooth walke the Meades,
        though *Coridon* be he that mowes them.
The little Lambs are *Phillis* love.
        though *Coridon* is he that feedes them:

[handwritten marginalia: form of "constant test"]

The Gardens faire are *Phillis* ground,
        though *Coridon* be he that weedes them.
Since then that *Phillis* onely is,
        the onely Sheepheards onely Queene:
And *Coridon* the onely Swaine,
        that onely hath her Sheepheard beene.
Though *Phillis* keepe her bower of state,
        shall *Coridon* consume away:
No Sheepheard no, worke out the weeke,
        And Sunday shall be holy-day.

N. Breton

owes] possesses

The passionate Sheepheards Song

ON a day, (alack the day,)
Love whose moneth was ever May:
Spied a blossome passing faire,
Playing in the wanton ayre.
Through the velvet leaves the wind,
All unseene gan passage find:
That the Sheepheard (sicke to death,)
Wish'd himselfe the heavens breath.
Ayre (quoth he) thy cheekes may blow,
Ayre, would I might triumph so.
But alas, my hand hath sworne,
Nere to pluck thee from thy thorne.
Vow (alack) for youth unmeete,
Youth so apt to pluck a sweete.
Thou for whom *Jove* would sweare,
Juno but an Æthiope were,
And deny him selfe for *Jove*,
Turning mortall for thy Love.

W. Shakespeare

53

The unknowne Sheepheards complaint

MY Flocks feede not, my Ewes breede not,
My Rammes speede not, all is amisse:
Love is denying, Faith is defying,
Harts renying, causer of this.
All my merry Jiggs are quite forgot,
All my Ladies love is lost God wot.
Where her faith was firmely fixt in love,
There a nay is plac'd without remove.
 One silly crosse, wrought all my losse,
 O frowning Fortune, cursed fickle Dame:
 For now I see, inconstancie
 More in women then in men remaine.

In black mourne I, all feares scorne I,
Love hath forlorne me, living in thrall:
Hart is bleeding, all helpe needing,
O cruell speeding, fraughted with gall.
My Sheepheards pipe can sound no deale,
My Weathers bell rings dolefull knell.
My curtaile dogge that wont to have plaide,
Playes not at all, but seemes afraide.
 With sighs so deepe, procures to weepe,
 In howling-wise, to see my dolefull plight:
 How sighs resound, through hartlesse ground,
 Like a thousand vanquish'd men in bloody
  fight.

Cleare Wells spring not, sweet birds sing not,
Greene plants bring not foorth their die:
Heards stand weeping, Flocks all sleeping,
Nimphs back peeping fearefully.
All our pleasure knowne to us poore Swaines,
All our merry meeting on the Plaines.
All our evening sports from us are fled,
All our love is lost, for Love is dead.

Farewell sweete Love, thy like nere was,
For sweete content, the cause of all my moane:
Poore *Coridon* must live alone,
Other helpe for him, I see that there is none.

Ignoto

renying] refusing

Another of the same Sheepheards

As it fell upon a day,
In the merry moneth of May,
Sitting in a pleasant shade,
Which a grove of Mirtles made.
Beasts did leape, and birds did sing,
Trees did grow, and plants did spring.
Every thing did banish moane,
Save the Nightingale alone.
Shee poore bird, as all forlorne,
Lean'd her breast against a thorne,
And there sung the dolefull'st Ditty,
That to heare it was great pitty.
Fie, fie, fie, now would she crie
Teru, Teru, by and by.
That to heare her so complaine,
Scarse I could from teares refraine.
For her greefes so lively showne,
Made me thinke upon mine owne.
Ah (thought I) thou mourn'st in vaine,
None takes pitty on thy paine.
Sencelesse trees, they cannot heare thee,
Ruthlesse beasts, they will not cheere thee.
King *Pandion* he is dead,
All thy friends are lapt in Lead.

All thy fellow birds doo sing,
Carelesse of thy sorrowing.
Even so poore bird like thee,
None a-live will pitty mee.

Ignoto

The Sheepheards allusion of his owne amorous infelicitie, to the offence of Actæon

ACTÆON lost in middle of his sport
Both shape and life, for looking but awry:
Diana was afraide he would report
What secrets he had seene in passing by.
   To tell but truth, the selfe same hurt have I:
   By viewing her for whom I daily die.
I leese my wonted shape, in that my mind
Dooth suffer wrack upon the stonie rock
Of her disdaine, who contrarie to kind
Dooth beare a breast more hard than any stock;
   And former forme of limbs is changed
    quite:
   By cares in love, and want of due delight.
I leese my life, in that each secret thought,
Which I conceave through wanton fond regard:
Dooth make me say, that life availeth nought,
Where service cannot have a due reward.
   I dare not name the Nimph that works my
    smart,
   Though Love hath grav'n her name within
    my hart.

Tho. Watson

leese] *lose*

Montanus *Sonnet to his faire* Phæbe

A TURTLE sate upon a leavelesse tree,
    Mourning her absent pheare,
    With sad and sorrie cheare.
    About her wondring stood,
    The Cittizens of wood.
    And whilst her plumes she rents,
    And for her Love laments:
    The stately trees complaine them,
    The birds with sorrow paine them.
    Each one that dooth her view,
    Her paines and sorrowes rue.
    But were the sorrowes knowne,
    That me hath over-throwne:
Or how would *Phæbe* sigh, if she did looke on mee?

The love-sicke *Polipheme* that could not see,
    Who on the barren shoare,
    His fortunes did deplore:
    And melteth all in mone,
    For *Galatea* gone,
    And with his cries
    Afflicts both earth and skies,
    And to his woe betooke,
    Dooth breake both pipe and hooke.
    For whom complaines the morne,
    For whom the Sea-Nimphs mourne.
    Alas his paine is nought,
    For were my woe but thought:
Oh how would *Phæbe* sigh, if she did looke on me?

    Beyond compare my paine,
        yet glad am I:
    If gentle *Phæbe* daine,
        to see her *Montan* die.

Thom. Lodge

pheare] *companion*

Phæbes *Sonnet, a replie to* Montanus *passion*

DOWNE a downe,
    Thus *Phillis* sung,
    By fancie once distressed:
Who so by foolish Love are stung
    are worthily oppressed.
    And so sing I, with downe a downe, &c.

When Love was first begot,
And by the mothers will:
Did fall to humane lot,
His solace to fulfill.
Devoide of all deceite,
A chast and holy fire:
Did quicken mans conceite,
And womens breasts inspire.
The Gods that saw the good,
That mortalls did approove:
With kind and holy moode,
Began to talke of Love.
    Downe a downe,
    Thus *Phillis* sung
    By fancie once distressed, &c.

But during this accord,
A wonder strange to heare:
Whilst Love in deede and word,
Most faithfull did appeare;
False semblance came in place,
By Jealousie attended:
And with a double face,
Both love and fancie blended.
Which made the Gods forsake,
And men from fancie flie;
And Maydens scorne a make,
Forsooth and so will I.

Downe a downe,
  Thus *Phillis* sung,
   By fancie once distressed:
Who so by foolish Love are stung,
  Are worthily oppressed.
And so sing I, with downe a downe, &c.

      Thom. Lodge

make] mate

Coridons *supplication to* Phillis

SWEETE *Phillis*, if a silly Swaine,
   may sue to thee for grace:
See not thy loving Sheepheard slaine,
   with looking on thy face.
But thinke what power thou hast got,
   upon my Flock and mee:
Thou seest they now regard me not,
   but all doo follow thee.
And if I have so farre presum'd,
   with prying in thine eyes:
Yet let not comfort be consum'd,
   that in thy pitty lyes.
But as thou art that *Phillis* faire,
   that Fortune favour gives:
So let not Love dye in despaire,
   that in they favour lives.
The Deere doo brouse upon the bryer,
   the birds doo pick the cherries:
And will not Beauty graunt Desire,
   one handfull of her berries?
If it be so that thou has sworne,
   that none shall looke on thee:

Yet let me know thou doost not scorne,
        to cast a looke on mee.
But if thy beauty make thee proude,
        thinke then what is ordain'd:
The heavens have never yet alow'd,
        that Love should be disdain'd.
Then least the Fates that favour Love,
        should curse thee for unkind:
Let me report for thy behoove,
        the honour of thy mind.
Let *Coridon* with full consent,
        set downe what he hath seene:
That *Phillida* with Loves content,
        is sworne the Sheepheards Queene.

                  N. Breton

Damætas *Madrigall in praise of his* Daphnis

Tune on my pipe the praises of my Love,
        Love faire and bright:
Fill earth with sound, and ayrie heavens above,
        heaven's *Joves* delight,
        with *Daphnis* praise.

To pleasant *Tempe* Groves and Plaines about,
        Plaines, Sheepheards pride:
Resounding Ecchoes of her praise ring out,
        ring farre and wide.
        my *Daphnis* praise.

When I begin to sing, begin to sound,
              sounds loud and shrill:
Doo make each note unto the skies rebound,
              skies calme and still,
                  with *Daphnis* praise.

Her tresses are like wiers of beaten gold,
              Gold bright and sheene:
Like *Nysus* golden haire that *Scilla* pold,
              Scill, ore-seene
                  through *Minos* love.

Her eyes like shining Lamps in midst of night,
              Night darke and dead:
Or as the Starres that give the Sea-men light,
              Light for to leade
                  their wandring Ships.

Amidst her cheekes the Rose and Lilly strive,
              Lilly, snow-white:
When their contend dooth make their colour thrive.
              Colour too bright
                  for Sheepheards eyes.

Her lips like Scarlet of the finest die,
              Scarlet blood-red:
Teeth white as Snow, which on the hills dooth lie,
              Hills over-spread
                  by Winters force.

Her skinne as soft as is the finest silke,
              Silke soft and fine:
Of colour like unto the whitest milke,
              Milke of the Kine
                  of *Daphnis* Heard.

As swift of foote as is the pretty Roe,
　　　Roe swift of pace:
When yelping Hounds pursue her to and fro,
　　　Hounds fierce in chase,
　　　　to reave her life.

Cease tongue to tell of any more compares,
　　　Compares too rude:
Daphnis deserts and beauty are too rare,
　　　Then heere conclude
　　　　faire *Daphnis* praise.

J. Wootton

pold] *sheared*

Dorons *description of his faire Sheepheardesse* Samela

LIKE to *Diana* in her Sommer weede,
Girt with a Crimson roabe of brightest die:
　　　goes faire *Samela*.
Whiter then be the flocks that stragling feed,
When wash'd by *Arethusa*, faint they lie,
　　　is faire *Samela*.
As faire *Aurora* in her morning gray,
Deckt with the ruddy glister of her love:
　　　is faire *Samela*.
Like lovely *Thetis* on a calmed day,
When as her brightnes *Neptunes* fancies move,
　　　shines faire *Samela*.
Her tresses gold, her eyes like glassie streames,
Her teeth are pearle, the brests are Ivorie:
　　　of faire *Samela*.
Her cheekes like Rose and Lilly yeeld foorth gleames,

62

Her browes bright arches fram'd of Ebonie,
                    thus faire *Samela*
Passeth faire *Venus* in her brightest hew,
And *Juno* in the shew of Majestie:
                    for she's *Samela*.
Pallas in wit, all three if you well view,
For beauty, wit, and matchlesse dignitie,
                    yeeld to *Samela*.

                                        Ro. Greene

Wodenfrides *Song in praise of* Amargana

THE Sunne the season in each thing
Revives new pleasures, the sweet Spring
Hath put to flight the Winter keene:
To glad our lovely Sommer Queene.

The pathes where *Amargana* treads,
With flowrie tap'stries *Flora* spreads.
And Nature cloathes the ground in greene:
To glad our lovely Sommer Queene.

The Groaves put on their rich aray,
With Hawthorne bloomes imbroydered gay,
And sweet perfum'd with Eglantine:
To glad our lovely Sommer Queene.

The silent River stayes his course,
Whilst playing on the christall sourse,
The silver scaled fish are seene,
To glad our lovely Sommer Queene.

The Woods at her faire sight rejoyces,
The little birds with their lowd voyces,
In consort on the bryers beene,
To glad our lovely Sommer Queene.

The fleecie Flocks doo scud and skip,
The wood-Nimphs, Fawnes, and Satires trip,
And daunce the Mirtle trees betweene:
To glad our lovely Sommer Queene.

Great *Pan* (our God) for her deere sake,
This feast and meeting bids us make,
Of Sheepheards, Lads, and Lasses sheene:
To glad our lovely Sheepheards Queene.

And every Swaine his chaunce dooth prove,
To winne faire *Amarganaes* love,
In sporting strifes quite voide of spleene:
To glad our lovely Sommer Queene.

All happiness let Heaven her lend,
And all the Graces her attend.
Thus bid me pray the Muses nine,
Long live our lovely Sommer Queene.

W. H.

Another of the same

HAPPY Sheepheards sit and see,
with joy,
The peerelesse wight:
For whose sake Pan keepes from ye
annoy,
And gives delight.

64

Blessing this pleasant Spring,
Her praises must I sing.
List you Swaines, list to me:
The whiles your Flocks feeding be.

First her brow a beauteous Globe,
I deeme,
And golden haire;
And her cheeke *Auroraes* roabe,
dooth seeme,
But farre more faire.
Her eyes like starres are bright.
And dazle with their light,
Rubies her lips to see,
But to tast, Nectar they be.

Orient pearles her teeth, her smile
dooth linke
the Graces three:
Her white necke dooth eyes beguile
to thinke
it Ivorie.
Alas her Lilly-hand,
How it dooth me commaund?
Softer silke none can be:
And whiter milke none can see.

Circes wand is not so straite,
as is
Her body small:
But two pillers beare the waight
of this
majestick Hall.
Those be I you assure,
Of Alablaster pure,
Polish's fine in each part:
Ne're Nature yet shewed like Art.

How shall I her pretty tread
        expresse
  when she dooth walke?
Scarse she dooth the Primrose head
        depresse,
  or tender stalke
  Of blew-veind Violets,
  Whereon her foote she sets.
  Vertuous she is, for we finde
  In body faire, beauteous minde.

Live faire *Amargana* still
        extold
  In all my rime:
Hand want Art, when I want will
        t'unfold
  her woorth divine.
  But now my Muse dooth rest,
  Dispaire clos'd in my brest,
  Of the valour I sing:
  Weake faith that no hope dooth bring.

W. H.

An excellent Pastorall Dittie

A CAREFULL Nimph, with carelesse greefe opprest,
  under the shaddow of an Ashen tree:
With Lute in hand did paint out her unrest,
  unto a Nimph that bare her companie.
    No sooner had she tuned every string:
    But sob'd and sigh'd, and thus began to sing.

Ladies and Nimphs, come listen to my plaint,
  on whom the cheerefull Sunne did never rise:

If pitties stroakes your tender breasts may taint,
   come learne of me to wet your wanton eyes.
      For Love in vaine the name of pleasure beares:
      His sweet delights are turned into feares.

The trustlesse shewes, the frights, the feeble joyes,
   the freezing doubts, the guilefull promises:
The feigned lookes, the shifts, the subtill toyes,
   the brittle hope, the steadfast heavines.
      The wished warre in such uncertaine peace:
      These with my woe, my woes with these increase.

Thou dreadfull God, that in thy Mothers lap,
   doo'st lye and heare the crie of my complaint,
And seest, and smilest at my sore mishap,
   that lacke but skill my sorrowes heere to paint:
      They fire from heaven before the hurt I spide,
      Quite through mine eyes into my brest did glide.

My life was light, my blood did spirt and spring,
   my body quicke, my hart began to leape:
And every thornie thought did prick and sting,
   the fruite of my desired joyes to reape.
      But he on whom to thinke, my soule still tyres:
      In bale forsooke, and left me in the bryers.

Thus Fancie strung my Lute to Layes of Love,
   and Love hath rock'd my wearie Muse a-sleepe:
And sleepe is broken by the paines I prove,
   and every paine I feele dooth force me weepe,
      Then farewell fancie, love, sleepe, paine, and sore:
      And farewell weeping, I can waile no more.

Shep. Tonie

Phillidaes *Love-call to her* Coridon, *and his replying*

Phil. CORIDON, arise my *Coridon*,
　　　Titan shineth cleare:
Cor. Who is it that calleth *Coridon*,
　　　who is it that I heare?
Phil. Phillida thy true-Love calleth thee,
　　　arise then, arise then;
　　　　arise and keepe thy flock with me:
Cor. Phillida my true-Love, is it she?
　　　I come then, I come then,
　　　　I come and keepe my flock with thee.

Phil. Heere are cherries ripe my *Coridon*,
　　　eate them for my sake:
Cor. Heere's my Oaten pipe my lovely one,
　　　sport for thee to make.
Phil. Heere are threeds my true-Love, fine as silke,
　　　to knit thee, to knit thee
　　　　a paire of stockings white as milke.
Cor. Heere are Reedes my true-Love, fine and neate,
　　　to make thee, to make thee
　　　　a Bonnet to with-stand the heate.

Phil. I will gather flowers my *Coridon*,
　　　to set in thy cap:
Cor. I will gather Peares my lovely one,
　　　to put in thy lap.
Phil. I will buy my true-Love Garters gay,
　　　for Sundayes, for Sundayes,
　　　　to weare about his legs so tall:
Cor. I will buy my true-Love yellow Say,
　　　for Sundayes, for Sundayes,
　　　　to weare about her middle small.

Phil. When my *Coridon* sits on a hill,
      making melodie:
Cor. When my lovely one goes to her wheele
      singing cherilie.
Phil. Sure me thinks my true-Love dooth excell
      for sweetnes, for sweetnes,
        our *Pan* that old Arcadian Knight:
Cor. And me thinks my true-Love beares the bell
      for clearenes, for clearenes,
        beyond the Nimphs that be so bright.

Phil. Had my *Coridon*, my *Coridon*,
      beene (alack) my Swaine:
Cor. Had my lovely one, my lovely one,
      beene in *Ida* plaine.
Phil. *Cinthia Endimion* had refus'd,
      preferring, preferring
        my *Coridon* to play with-all:
Cor. The Queene of Love had beene excus'd,
      bequeathing, bequeathing,
        my *Phillida* the golden ball.

Phil. Yonder comes my Mother, *Coridon*,
      whether shall I flie?
Cor. Under yonder Beech my lovely one,
      while she passeth by.
Say to her thy true-Love was not heere,
      remember, remember,
        to morrow is another day:
Phil. Doubt me not, my true-Love, doo not feare,
      farewell then, farewell then,
        heaven keepe our loves alway.

                            Ignoto

The Sheepheards solace

PHÆBUS delights to view his Laurell tree,
The Poplar pleaseth *Hercules* alone:
Melissa mother is and fautrixe to the Bee,
Pallas will weare the Olive branch alone.
　　Of Sheepheards and their flocks *Pales* is Queene:
　　And *Ceres* ripes the Corne was lately greene.
To *Chloris* every flower belongs of right,
The *Dryade* Nimphs of woods make chiefe account:
Oreades in hills have their delight,
Dianna dooth protect each bubling Fount.
　　To *Hebe* lovely kissing is assign'd:
　　To *Zephire* every gentle-breathing wind.
But what is Loves delight? To hurt each where
He cares not whom, with Darts of deepe desire:
With watchfull jealousie, with hope, with feare,
With nipping cold, and secret flames of fire.
　　O happy houre, wherein I did forgoe:
　　This little God, so great a cause of woe.

Tho. Watson

fautrixe] feminine of *fautor*, supporter, *patroness*

Syrenus *Song to* Eugerius

LET now the goodly Spring-tide make us merrie,
　　And fields, which pleasant flowers doo adorne:
　　And Vales, Meades, Woods, with lively colours
　　　　flourish,
Let plenteous flocks the Sheepheards riches nourish,
　　Let hungry Woolves by dogges to death be torne,
　　And Lambes rejoyce, with passed winter wearie.
　　　　Let every Rivers Ferrie
　　　　In waters flow, and silver streames abounding,
　　　　And fortune, ceaseless wounding.

Turne now thy face, so cruell and unstable,
    Be firme and favourable.
And thou that kill'st our soules with thy
        pretences:
Molest not (wicked Love) my inward sences.

Let Country plainenes live in joyes not ended,
  In quiet of the desert Meades and mountaines,
  And in the pleasure of a Country dwelling
Let Sheepheards rest, that have distilled fountaines
  Of teares: proove not thy wrath, all paines
        excelling,
Upon poore soules, that never have offended.
     Let thy flames be incended
  In haughtie Courts, in those that swim in
        treasure,
     And live in ease and pleasure.
And that a sweetest scorne (my wonted sadnes)
    A perfect rest and gladnes
And hills and Dales, may give me: with offences
Molest not (wicked Love) my inward sences.

In what law find'st thou, that the freest reason
  And wit, unto thy chaines should be subjected,
  And harmelesse soules unto thy cruell murder?
O wicked Love, the wretch that flieth furder
  From thy extreames, thou plagu'st. O false,
        suspected,
  And carelesse boy, that thus thy sweets doost
        season,
     O vile and wicked treason.
  Might not thy might suffise thee, but thy fuell
    Of force must be so cruell?
  To be a Lord, yet like a Tyrant minded,
    Vaine boy with errour blinded.
  Why doost thou hurt his life with thy offences:
That yeelds to thee his soule and inward sences?

71

He erres (alas) and foulely is deceaved
  That calls thee God, being a burning fire:
    A furious flame, a playning greefe and clamorous,
And *Venus* sonne (that in the earth was amorous,
  Gentle, and mild, and full of sweet desire)
  Who calleth him, is of his wits bereaved.
      And yet that she conceaved
    By proofe, so vile a sonne and so unruly:
      I say (and yet say truly)
    That in the cause of harmes, that they have
      framed,
      Both justly may be blamed:
  She that did breede him with such vile pretences,
  He that dooth hurt so much our inward sences.

The gentle Sheepe and Lambs are ever flying
  The ravenous Woolves and beasts, that are
    pretending
  To glut their mawes with flesh they teare asunder.
The milke-white Doves at noyse of fearefull thunder
  Flie home a-maine, themselves from harme
    defending.
  The little Chick, when Puttocks are a crying,
    The Woods and Meadowes dying
    For raine of heaven (if that they cannot have it)
      Doo never cease to crave it.
  So every thing his contrary resisteth,
    Onely thy thrall persisteth
  In suffering of thy wrongs without offences:
  And lets thee spoile his hart and inward sences.

A publique passion, Natures lawes restrayning,
  And which with words can never be declared,
  A soule twixt love, and feare, and desperation,
And endlesse plaint, that shuns all consolation,
  A spendlesse flame, that never is impaired,

A friendlesse death, yet life in death maintayning,
A passion, that is gayning
On him that loveth well, and is absented,
Whereby it is augmented.
A jealousie, a burning greefe and sorrow,
These favours Lovers borrow
Of thee fell Love, these be thy recompences:
Consuming still their soule and inward sences.

Bar. Yong

Puttocks] *kites*—the bird was common in 1600

The Sheepheard Arsileus *replie to* Syrenus *Song*

O LET that time a thousand moneths endure,
Which brings from heaven the sweet and silver
showers,
And joyes the earth (of comfort late deprived)
With grasse and leaves, fine buds, and painted
flowers.
Ecchoe, returne unto the woods obscure.
Ring forth the Sheepheards Songs in love
contrived.
Let old loves be revived,
Which angry Winter buried but of late,
And that in such a state
My soule may have the full accomplishment
Of joy and sweet content.
And since fierce paines and greefes thou doost
controule:
Good Love, doo not forsake my inward soule.

Presume not (Sheepheards) once to make you merrie,
With springs, and flowers, or any pleasant Song,
(Unlesse mild Love possesse your amorous breasts)
    If you sing not to him, your Songs doo wearie,
    Crowne him with flowers, or else ye doo him
                  wrong,
    And consecrate your Springs to his behests.
            I to my Sheepheardesse
  My happy loves with great content doo sing.
        And flowers to her doo bring.
  And sitting neere her by the River side,
        Enjoy the brave Spring-tide.
  Since then thy joyes such sweetnes dooth
          enroule:
  Good Love, doo not forsake my inward soule.

The wise (in auncient time) a God thee nam'd,
Seeing that with they power and supreame might,
Thou didst such rare and mighty wonders make:
    For thee a hart is frozen and enflam'd,
    A foole thou mak'st a wise man with thy light,
    The coward turnes couragious for thy sake.
           The mighty Gods did quake
  At thy commaund: To birds and beasts
         transformed,
        Great Monarches have not scorned
  To yeeld unto the force of beauties lure:
        Such spoiles thou doost procure
  With thy brave force, which never may be tould:
  With which (sweet Love) thou conquer'st every
         soule.

In other times obscurely I did live
But with a drowsie, base, and simple kinde
Of life, and onely to my profit bend me:
    To thinke of Love my selfe I did not give,
    Or for good grace, good parts, and gentle minde,
    Never did any Sheepheardesse commend me.
           But crowned now they send me

A thousand Garlands, that I wone with praise,
        In wrastling dayes by dayes,
In pitching of the barre with arme most strong,
        And singing many a Song.
After that thou didst honour, and take hould
Of me (sweet Love) and of my happy soule.

What greater joy can any man desire,
Then to remaine a Captive unto Love:
And have his hart subjected to his power?
    And though sometimes he tast a little sower
    By suffering it, as mild as gentle Dove
Yet must he be, in liew of that great hire
        Whereto he dooth aspire:
If Lovers live afflicted and in paine,
        Let them with cause complaine
Of cruell fortune, and of times abuse,
        And let not them accuse
Thee (gentle-Love) that dooth with blisse enfould
Within thy sweetest joyes each living soule.

Behold a faire sweete face, and shining eyes,
Resembling two most bright and twinkling starres,
Sending unto the soule a perfect light:
    Behold the rare perfections of those white
    An Ivorie hands, from greefes most surest barres:
That mind wherein all life and glory lyes,
        That joy that never dyes,
That he dooth feele, that loves and is beloved,
        And my delights approoved,
To see her pleas'd, whose love maintaines me
        heere,
        All those I count so deere,
That though sometimes Love dooth my joyes
        controule:
Yet am I glad he dwels within my soule.

                       Bar. Yong

hire] *reward*

A Sheepheards dreame

A SILLY Sheepheard lately sate
      among a flock of Sheepe:
Where musing long on this and that,
      at last he fell a sleepe.
And in the slumber as he lay,
      he gave a pitteous groane:
He thought his sheepe were runne away,
      and he was left alone.
He whoopt, he whistled, and he call'd,
      but not a sheepe came neere him:
Which made the Sheepheard sore appall'd,
      to see that none would heare him.
But as the Swaine amazed stood,
      in this most solemne vaine:
Came *Phillida* foorth of the wood,
      and stoode before the Swaine.
Whom when the Sheepheard did behold,
      he straite began to weepe:
And at the hart he grew a cold,
      to thinke upon his sheepe.
For well he knew, where came the Queene,
      the Sheepheard durst not stay:
And where that he durst not be seene,
      the sheepe must needes away.
To aske her if she saw his flock,
      might happen pacience moove:
And have an aunswere with a mock,
      that such demaunders proove.
Yet for because he saw her come
      alone out of the wood:
He thought he would not stand as dombe,
      when speach might doo him good.
And therefore falling on his knees,
      to aske but for his sheepe:
He did awake, and so did leese
      the honour of his sleepe.   *N. Breton*

The Sheepheards Ode

NIGHTS were short, and dayes were long,
Blossomes on the Hawthorne hong,
Philomell (Night-Musiques King,)
Told the comming of the Spring:
Whose sweete-silver-sounding-voyce,
Made the little birds rejoyce,
Skipping light from spray to spray,
Till *Aurora* shew'd the day.
Scarse might one see, when I might see
(For such chaunces sudden be)
By a Well of Marble-stone,
A Sheepheard lying all a-lone.
Weepe he did, and his weeping
Made the fading flowers spring.
Daphnis was his name I weene,
Youngest Swaine of Sommers Queene.
When *Aurora* saw t'was he
Weepe she did for companie:
Weepe she did for her sweet Sonne,
That (when antique Troy was wonne)
Suffer'd death by lucklesse Fate,
Whom she now laments too late:
And each morning (by Cocks crewe)
Showers downe her silver dewe,
Whose teares falling from their spring,
Give moisture to each living thing
That on earth encrease and grow,
Through power of their friendly foe.
Whose effect when *Flora* felt,
Teares, that did her bosome melt,
(For who can resist teares often,
But she whom no teares can soften?)
Peering straite above the banks,
Shew'd her selfe to give her thanks.
Wondring thus at Natures worke
(Wherein many mervailes lurke)

77

Me thought I heard a dolefull noyse,
Consorted with a mournfull voyce,
Drawing neere, to heare more plaine,
Heare I did, unto my paine,
(For who is not pain'd to heare
Him in grief whom hart holds deere?)
Silly Swaine with griefe ore-gone
Thus to make his pitteous mone.
Love I did, alas the while,
Love I did, but did beguile
My deere Love with loving so,
Whom as then I did not know.
Love I did the fayrest boy
That these fields did ere enjoy
Love I did faire *Ganimede*,
Venus darling, beauties bed:
Him I thought the fairest creature,
Him the quintessence of Nature.
But yet (alas) I was deceav'd,
(Love of reason is bereav'd.)
For since then I saw a Lasse,
Lasse that did in beauty passe,
Passe faire *Ganimede* as farre
As *Phœbus* dooth the smallest starre.
Love commaunded me to love,
Fancie bad me not remove
My affection from the Swaine
Whom I never could obtaine:
(For who can obtaine that favour
Which he cannot graunt the craver?)
Love at last (though loth) prevail'd,
Love that so my heart assail'd,
Wounding me with her faire eyes
Ah how Love can subtillize?
And devise a thousand shifts
How to worke men to his drifts.
Her it is, for whom I mourne,
Her, for whom my life I scorne.

Her, for whom I weepe all day,
Her, for whom I sigh, and say
Eyther she, or else no creature
Shall enjoy my love: whose feature
Though I never can obtaine,
Yet shall my true-love remaine:
Till (my body turn'd to clay)
My poore soule must passe away,
To the heavens; where I hope
It shall finde a resting scope.
Then since I loved thee alone,
Remember me when I am gone.
Scarce had he these last words spoken,
But me thought his hart was broken,
With great greefe that did abound,
(Cares and greefe the hart confound.)
In whose hart thus riv'd in three,
Eliza written I might see
In Caracters of crimson blood,
Whose meaning well I understood.
Which, for my hart might not behold:
I hied me home my Sheepe to fold.

Rich. Barnefielde

The Sheepheards commendation of his Nimph

WHAT Sheepheard can expresse
The favour of her face?
To whom in this distresse
I doo appeale for grace.
    A thousand *Cupids* flye
    About her gentle eye.

From which each throwes a dart,
That kindleth soft sweet fire
Within my sighing hart,
Possessed by desire.
 No sweeter life I trie
 Then in her love to die.

The Lilly in the field,
That glories in his white:
For purenes now must yeeld
And render up his right.
 Heaven pictur'd in her face,
 Dooth promise joy and grace.

Faire *Cinthiaes* silver light,
That beates on running streames:
Compares not with her white,
Whose haires are all Sunne-beames.
 So bright my Nimph dooth shine
 As day unto my eyne.

With this there is a red,
Exceedes the Damaske-Rose:
Which in her cheekes is spred,
Whence every favour growes.
 In Skie there is no starre,
 But she surmounts it farre.

When *Phœbus* from the bed
Of *Thetis* dooth arise;
The morning blushing red,
In faire Carnation wise:
 He shewes in my Nimphs face,
 As Queene of every grace.

This pleasant Lilly white,
This taint of Roseate red:
This *Cinthiaes* silver light,
This sweete faire Dea spred,
    These Sun-beames in mine eye,
    These beauties make me die.

Earle of Oxenford

Coridon *to his* Phillis

ALAS my hart, mine eye hath wronged thee,
Presumptuous eye, to gaze on *Phillis* face:
Whose heavenly eye no mortall man may see,
But he must die, or purchase *Phillis* grace.
    Poore *Coridon*, the Nimph whose eye dooth
        moove thee:
    Dooth love to draw, but is not drawne to love
        thee.
Her beautie, Natures pride, and Sheepheards praise,
Her eye, the heavenly Planet of my life:
Her matchlesse wit and grace, her fame displaies,
As if that *Jove* had made her for his wife.
    Onely her eyes shoote fierie darts to kill:
    Yet is her hart as cold as *Caucase* hill.
My wings too weake to flye against the Sunne,
Mine eyes unable to sustaine her light:
My hart dooth yeeld that I am quite undone,
Thus hath faire *Phillis* slaine me with her sight.
    My bud is blasted, withred is my leafe:
    And all my corne is rotted in the sheafe.
Phillis, the golden fetter of my minde,
My fancies Idoll, and my vitall power:
Goddesse of Nimphs, and honour of thy kinde,
This ages *Phœnix*, beauties richest bower.

Poore *Coridon* for love of thee must die:
Thy beauties thrall, and conquest of thine
eye.
Leave *Coridon* to plough the barren field,
Thy buds of hope are blasted with disgrace:
For *Phillis* lookes no harty love doo yeeld,
Nor can she love, for all her lovely face.
Die *Coridon*, the spoile of *Phillis* eye:
She cannot love, and therefore thou must die.

S. E. Dyer

The Sheepheards description of Love

Melibeus. SHEEPHEARD, what's Love, I pray thee tell?
Faustus. It is that Fountaine, and that Well,
Where pleasure and repentance dwell.
It is perhaps that saucing bell,
That toules all into heaven or hell,
And this is Love as I heard tell.
Meli. Yet what is Love, I pre-thee say?
Fau. It is a worke on holy-day,
It is December match'd with May,
When lustie-bloods in fresh aray,
Heare ten moneths after of the play,
And this is Love, as I heare say.
Meli. Yet what is Love, good Sheepheard saine?
Fau. It is a Sun-shine mixt with raine,
It is a tooth-ach, or like paine,
It is a game where none dooth gaine,
The Lasse saith no, and would full
faine:
And this is Love, as I heare saine.
Meli. Yet Sheepheard, what is Love, I pray?
Fau. It is a yea, it is a nay,

82

A pretty kind of sporting fray,
It is a thing will soone away,
    Then Nimphs take vantage while ye
    may:
  And this is love as I heare say.
Meli. Yet what is love, good Sheepheard show?
Fau. A thing that creepes, it cannot goe,
A prize that passeth too and fro,
A thing for one, a thing for moe,
    And he that prooves shall finde it so;
    And Sheepheard this is love I troe.

                        Ignoto

sauncing bell] Sanctus bell

To his Flocks

FEEDE on my Flocks securely,
Your Sheepheard watcheth surely,
Runne about my little Lambs,
Skip and wanton with your Dammes,
    Your loving Heard with care will tend ye:
Sport on faire flocks at pleasure,
Nip *Vestaes* flowring treasure,
I my selfe will duely harke,
When my watchfull dogge dooth barke,
    From Woolfe and Foxe I will defend ye.

                        H. C.

A Roundelay between two Sheepheards

1. *Shep.* TELL me thou gentle Sheepheards Swaine,
    Who'se yonder in the Vale is set?
2. *Shep.* Oh it is she, whose sweetes doo staine,
    The Lilly, Rose, the Violet.

1. *Shep.* Why dooth the Sunne against his kind,
    Fixe his bright Chariot in the skies?
2. *Shep.* Because the Sunne is strooken blind,
    With looking on her heavenly eyes.

1. *Shep.* Why doo thy flocks forbeare their food,
    Which sometime were thy chiefe delight?
2. *Shep.* Because they neede no other good,
    That live in presence of her sight.

1. *Shep.* Why looke these flowers so pale and ill,
    That once attir'd this goodly Heath?
2. *Shep.* She hath rob'd Nature of her skill,
    And sweetens all things with her breath.

1. *Shep.* Why slide these brookes so slow away,
    Whose bubling murmur pleas'd thine eare?
2. *Shep.* Oh mervaile not although they stay,
    When they her heavenly voyce doo heare.

1. *Shep.* From whence come all these Sheepheards
        Swaines,
    And lovely Nimphs attir'd in greene?
2. *Shep.* From gathering Garlands on the Plaines,
    To crowne our faire the Sheepheards Queene.

Both. The Sunne that lights this world below,
    Flocks, flowers, and brookes will witnesse
        beare:
    These Nimphs and Sheepheards all doo know,
    That it is she is onely faire.

Mich. Drayton

The solitarie Sheepheards Song

O SHADIE Vales, ô faire enriched Meades,
    O sacred woods, sweet fields, and rising moun-
        taines:
O painted flowers, greene hearbs where *Flora* treads,
    Refresht by wanton winds and watry foun-
        taines.

O all you winged Queristers of wood,
    that pearcht aloft, your former paines report:
And straite againe recount with pleasant moode,
    your present joyes in sweete and seemely sort.

O all you creatures whosoever thrive
    on mother earth, in Seas, by ayre, by fire:
More blest are you then I heere under Sunne,
    love dies in me, when as he dooth revive
In you, I perish under beauties ire,
    where after stormes, winds, frosts, your life is
        wunne.

Thom. Lodge

The Sheepheards resolution in love

IF *Jove* him-selfe be subject unto Love,
And range the woods to finde a mortall pray,
If *Neptune* from the Seas him-selfe remove,
And seeke on sands with earthly wights to play:
    Then may I love my Sheepheardesse by right,
    Who farre excells each other mortall wight?

If *Pluto* could by Love be drawne from hell,
To yeeld him-selfe a silly virgins thrall.
If *Phœbus* could vouchsafe on earth to dwell,
To winne a rustick Mayde unto his call:
    Then how much more should I adore the sight,
    Of her in whom the heavens them-selves delight?

If Country *Pan* might follow Nimphs in chase,
And yet through love remaine devoide of blame,
If *Satires* were excus'd for seeking grace,
To joy the fruites of any mortall Dame:
    My Sheepheardesse, why should not I love still
    On whom nor Gods nor men can gaze their fill?

Tho. Watson

Coridons *Hymne in praise of* Amarillis

WOULD mine eyes were christall Fountaines,
Where you might the shadow view
Of my greefes, like to these mountaines
Swelling for the losse of you.
Cares which curelesse are alas,
Helplesse, haplesse for they grow:
Cares like tares in number passe,
All the seedes that love dooth sow
Who but could remember all
Twinkling eyes still representing?
Starres which pierce me to the gall,
Cause they lend no more contenting.
And you Nectar-lips, alluring
Humane sence to tast of heaven:
For no Art of mans manuring,
Finer silke hath ever weaven.

Who but could remember this,
The sweete odours of your favour?
When I smeld I was in blisse,
Never felt I sweeter savour.
And your harmelesse hart annoynted,
As the custome was of Kings:
Shewes your sacred soule appoynted,
To be prime of earthly things.
Ending thus remember all,
Cloathed in a mantle greene:
Tis enough I am your thrall,
Leave to thinke what eye hath seene.
Yet the eye may not so leave,
Though the thought doo still repine:
But must gaze till death bequeath,
Eyes and thoughts unto her shrine.
Which if *Amarillis* chaunce,
Hearing to make hast to see:
To life death she may advaunce.
Therefore eyes and thoughts goe free.

T. B.

The Sheepheard Carillo *his Song*

> *Guarda mi las Vaccas*
> *Carillo, por tu fe,*
> *Besa mi Primero,*
> *Yo te las guardare.*

I PRE-THEE keepe my Kine for me
Carillo, wilt thou? Tell.
First let me have a kisse of thee,
And I will keepe them well.

87

If to my charge or them to keepe,
Thou doost commend thy Kine or Sheepe,
        For thee I doo suffise:
Because in this I have beene bred,
But for so much as I have fed
           By viewing thee, mine eyes;
       Commaund not me to keepe thy beast:
       Because my self I can keepe least.

How can I keepe, I pre-thee tell,
Thy Kie, my selfe that cannot well
           defend, nor please thy kinde,
As long as I have served thee?
But if thou wilt give unto me
          a kisse to please my minde:
       I aske no more for all my paine,
       And I will keepe them very faine.

For thee, the gift is not so great
That I doo aske, to keepe thy Neate,
         but unto me it is
A guerdon, that shall make me live.
Disdaine not then to lend or give
          so small a gift as this.
       But if to it thou canst not frame:
       Then give me leave to take the same.

But if thou doost (my sweet) denie
To recompence me by and by,
          thy promise shall relent me:
Heere-after some reward to finde,
Behold how I doo please my minde,
          and favours doo content me,
       That though thou speak'st it but in jest:
       I meane to take it at the best.

Behold how much love works in me,
And how ill recompenc'd of thee
          that with the shadow of
Thy happy favours (though delay'd)
I thinke my selfe right well appay'd,
           although they proove a scoffe.
    Then pity me, that have forgot:
    My selfe for thee, that carest not.

O in extreame thou art most faire,
And in extreame unjust despaire
          thy cruelty maintaines:
O that thou wert so pittifull
Unto these torments that doo pull
          my soule with sencelesse paines,
    As thou shew'st in that face of thine:
    Where pitty and mild grace should shine.

If that thy faire and sweetest face
Assureth me both peace and grace,
          thy hard and cruell hart:
Which in that white breast thou doo'st beare,
Dooth make me tremble yet for feare
          thou wilt not end my smart.
    In contraries of such a kinde:
    Tell me what succour shall I finde?

If then young Sheepheardesse thou crave
A Heards-man for thy beast to have,
          with grace thou maist restore
Thy Sheepheard from his barren love,
For never other shalt thou proove,
          that seekes to please thee more:
    And who to serve thy turne, will never shun,
    The nipping frost, and beames of parching
          Sun.

                        Bar. Yong

Kie] *Kine*   *faine*] *gladly*

Corins *dreame of his faire* Chloris

WHAT time bright *Titan* in the *Zenith* sat,
And equally the fixed poales did heate:
When to my flock my daily woes I chat,
And underneath a broade Beech tooke my seate.
The dreaming God which *Morpheus* Poets call
Augmenting fuell to my *Aetnaes* fire,
With sleepe possessing my weake sences all,
In apparitions makes my hopes aspire.
Me thought I saw the Nimph I would embrace,
With armes abroade comming to me for helpe:
A lust-led Satire having her in chace,
Which after her about the fields did yelpe.
I seeing my Love in such perplexed plight,
A sturdie bat from off an Oake I reft:
And with the Ravisher continued fight,
Till breathlesse I upon the earth him left.
Then when my coy Nimph saw her breathlesse foe,
With kisses kind she gratifies my paine:
Protesting rigour never more to show,
Happy was I this good hap to obtaine.
But drowsie slumbers flying to their Cell,
My sudden joy converted was to bale:
My wonted sorrowes still with me doo dwell,
I looked round about on hill and Dale:
But I could neither my faire *Chloris* view,
Nor yet the Satire which yer-while I slew.

W. S.

The Sheepheard Damons *passion*

Ah trees, why fall your leaves so fast?
Ah Rocks, where are your roabes of mosse?
Ah Flocks, why stand you all agast?
    Trees, Rocks, and Flocks, what, are ye pensive for
      my losse?

The birds me thinks tune naught but moane,
The winds breath naught but bitter plaint:
The beasts forsake their dennes to groane,
    Birds, winds and beasts what, dooth my
      losse your powers attaint?

Floods weepe their springs above their bounds,
And Eccho wailes to see my woe:
The roabe of ruthe dooth cloath the grounds,
    Floods, Eccho, grounds, why doo ye all these
      teares bestow?

The trees, the Rocks and Flocks replie,
The birds, the winds, the beasts report:
Floods, Eccho, grounds for sorrow crie,
    We greeve since *Phillis* nill kinde *Damons* love
      consort.

                      Thom. Lodge

The Sheepheard Musidorus *his complaint*

Come Sheepheards weedes, become your Maisters
    minde,
Yeeld outward shew, what inward change he tries:
Nor be abash'd, since such a guest you finde,
Whose strongest hope in your weake comfort lies.

Come Sheepheards weedes, attend my wofull cries,
Disuse your selves from sweete *Menalcas* voyce:
For other be those tunes which sorrow ties,
From those cleare notes which freely may rejoyce.
>   Then poure out plaints, and in one word say
>   this:
>   Helplesse his plaint, who spoiles him selfe of
>   blisse.

S. Phil. Sidney

The Sheepheards braule, one halfe aunswering the other

1. WE love, and have our loves rewarded?
2. We love, and are no whit regarded.
1. We finde most sweet affections snare:
2. That sweete but sower dispairefull care.
1. Who can dispaire, whom hope dooth beare?
2. And who can hope, that feeles dispaire?
All.   As without breath no pipe dooth move:
>   No Musique kindly without love.

S. Phil. Sidney

Dorus *his comparisons*

MY Sheepe are thoughts, which I both guide and
    serve,
Their pasture is faire hills of fruitless love:
On barren sweetes, they feede, and feeding sterve,
I waile their lot, but will not other prove.

My sheepe-hooke is wanne hope, which all upholds:
My weedes, desires, cut out in endlesse folds.
What wooll my Sheepe shall beare, while
thus they live:
In you it is, you must the judgement give.

S. Phil. Sidney

The Sheepheard Faustus *his Song*

A faire Mayde wed to prying Jealousie,
One of the fairest as ever I did see:
If that thou wilt a secret Lover take,
(Sweet life) doe not my secret love forsake.

ECCLIPSED was our Sunne,
And faire *Aurora* darkened to us quite,
Our morning starre was doone,
And Sheepheards starre lost cleane out of
our sight,
When that thou didst thy faith in wedlock
plight.
Dame Nature made thee faire,
And ill did carelesse Fortune marry thee,
And pitty with despaire
It was, that this thy haplesse hap should be
A faire Mayde wed to prying Jealousie.

Our eyes are not so bold
To view the Sun, that flies with radiant
wing:
Unlesse that we doo hold
A glasse before them, or some other thing.
Then wisely this to passe did Fortune bring
To cover thee with such a vaile:

                   For heeretofore, when any viewed thee,
Thy sight made his to faile,
                         For (sooth) thou art; thy beautie telleth
                               mee,
                         One of the fairest as ever I did see.

Thy graces to obscure,
                   With such a froward husband, and so base
She meant thereby most sure
                         That *Cupids* force, and love thou should'st
                               embrace,
                         For 'tis a force to love, no wondrous case.
Then care no more for kin,
                         And doubt no more, for feare thou must
                               forsake,
To love thou must begin,
                         And from hence-forth this question never
                               make,
                         If that thou should'st a secret Lover take?

Of force it dooth behoove
                         That thou should'st be belov'd, and that
                               againe
(Faire Mistresse) thou should'st love,
                         For to what end, what purpose, and what
                               gaine,
                         Should such perfections serve? as now in
                               vaine.
My love is of such art,
                         That (of it selfe) it well deserves to take
In thy sweete love a part:
                         Then for no Sheepheard, that his love
                               dooth make,
                         (Sweet life) doo not my secret love forsake.

                                             Bar. Yong

Another of the same, by Firmius
the Sheepheard

IF that the gentle winde
>>> dooth moove the leaves with pleasant
>>> sound,
If that the Kid behind
Is left, that cannot find
>>> her dam, runnes bleating up and downe:
The Bagpipe, Reede, or Flute,
>>> onely with ayre if that they touched be,
With pitty all salute,
And full of love doo brute
>>> thy name, and sound *Diana*, seeing thee:
>>> *A faire Mayde wed to prying Jealousie.*

The fierce and savage beasts
>>> (beyond their kind and nature yet)
With pitteous voyce and brest,
In mountaines without rest
>>> the selfe same Song doo not forget.
If that they stay'd at (*Faire*)
>>> and had not passed to prying *Jealousie*:
With plaints of such despaire
As moov'd the gentle ayre
>>> to teares: The Song that they did sing,
>>> should be
>>> *One of the fayrest as ever I did see.*

Mishap, and fortunes play,
>>> ill did they place in Beauties brest:
For since so much to say,
There was of beauties sway,
>>> they had done well to leave the rest.
They had enough to doo,
>>> if in her praise their wits they did awake:

But yet so must they too,
And all thy love that woo,
> thee not too coy, nor too too proude to
> make,
> *If that thou wilt a secret Lover take.*

For if thou hadst but knowne
> the beauty, that they heere doo touch,
Thou would'st then love alone
Thy selfe, nor any one,
> onely thy selfe accounting much.
But if thou doo'st conceave
> this beauty, that I will not publique make,
And mean'st not to bereave
The world of it, but leave
> the same to some (which never peere did
> take,)
> (*Sweet life*) *doo not my secret love forsake.*

Bar. Yong

Damelus *Song to his* Diaphenia

DIAPHENIA like the Daffadown-dillie,
White as the Sunne, faire as the Lillie,
> heigh hoe, how I doo love thee?
I doo love thee as my Lambs
Are beloved of their Dams,
> how blest were I if thou would'st proove
> me?

Diaphenia like the spreading Roses,
That in thy sweetes all sweetes incloses,
> faire sweete how I doo love thee?

I doo love thee as each flower,
Loves the Sunnes life-giving power.
> for dead, thy breath to life might move
> me.

Diaphenia like to all things blessed,
When all thy praises are expressed,
> deare Joy, how I doo love thee?
As the birds doo love the Spring:
Or the Bees their carefull King,
> then in requite, sweet Virgin love me.

                                H. C.

The Sheepheard Eurymachus to his faire Sheepheardesse Mirimida

WHEN Flora proud in pompe of all her flowers
> sate bright and gay:
And gloried in the dewe of Iris showers,
> and did display
Her mantle checquer'd all with gaudie greene,
> Then I
> alone
A mournfull man in Ericine was seene.

With folded armes I trampled through the grasse,
> Tracing as he
That held the throane of Fortune brittle glasse,
> And love to be
Like Fortune fleeting, as the restlesse wind
> Mixed
> with mists
Whose dampe dooth make the clearest eyes grow
> blind.

Thus in a maze, I spied a hideous flame,
                    I cast my sight,
And sawe where blithely bathing in the same
                    With great delight
A worme did lie, wrapt in a smoakie sweate:
                    And yet
                         twas strange,
It carelesse lay, and shrunk not at the heate.

I stoode amaz'd, and wondring at the sight,
                    while that a dame,
That shone like to the heavens rich sparkling light,
                    Discourst the same,
And said, My friend, this worme within the fire:
                    Which lyes
                         content,
Is *Venus* worme, and represents desire.

A Salamander is this princely beast,
                    Deck'd with a crowne,
Given him by *Cupid* as a gorgeous creast,
                    Gainst Fortunes frowne.
Content he lyes, and bathes him in the flame,
                    And goes
                         not foorth,
For why, he cannot live without the same.

As he, so Lovers live within the fire
                    Of fervent love:
And shrinke not from the flame of hote desire,
                    Nor will not move
From any heate that *Venus* force imparts:
                    But lie
                         content,
Within a fire, and waste away their harts.

Up flewe the Dame, and vanish'd in a cloud,
        But there stoode I,
And many thoughts within my mind did shroud
        My love: for why
I felt within my hart a scorching fire,
        And yet
        as did
The Salamander twas my whole desire.

Ro. Greene

The Sheepheard Firmius *his Song*

SHEEPHEARDS give eare, and now be still
Unto my passions and their cause,
        and what they be:
Since that with such an earnest will,
And such great signes of friendships lawes,
        you aske it me.

It is not long since I was whole,
Nor since I did in every part
        free-will resigne:
It is not long since in my sole
Possession, I did know my hart,
        and to be mine.

It is not long, since even and morrow,
All pleasure that my hart could finde,
        was in my power:
It is not long, since greefe and sorrow,
My loving hart began to binde,
        and to devoure.

It is not long, since companie
I did esteeme a joy indeede
      still to frequent:
Nor long, since solitarilie
I liv'd, and that this life did breede
      my sole content.

Desirous I (wretched) to see,
But thinking not to see so much
      as then I sawe:
Love made me know in what degree,
His valour and brave force did touch
      me with his lawe.

First he did put no more nor lesse
Into my hart, then he did view
      that there did want:
But when my breast in such excesse
Of lively flames to burne I knew,
      then were so scant

My joyes, that now did so abate,
(My selfe estraunged every way
      from former rest:)
That I did know, that my estate,
And that my life was every day,
      in deaths arrest.

I put my hand into my side,
To see what was the cause of this
      unwonted vaine:
Where I did finde, that torments hied
By endlesse death to prejudice
      my life with paine.

Because I sawe that there did want
My hart, wherein I did delight,
      my dearest hart:

100

And he that did the same supplant,
No jurisdiction had of right
      to play that part.

The Judge and Robber, that remaine
Within my soule, their cause to trie,
      are there all one:
And so the giver of the paine,
And he that is condemn'd to die
      or I, or none.

To die I care not any way,
Though without why, to die I greeve,
      as I doo see:
But for because I heard her say,
None die for love, for I beleeve
      none such there be.

Then this thou shalt beleeve by me
Too late, and without remedie
      as did in briefe:
Anaxarete, and thou shalt see,
The little she did satisfie
      with after griefe.

                     Bar. Yong

The Sheepheards praise of his sacred Diana

PRAYSED be *Dianaes* faire and harmlesse light,
Praised be the dewes, where-with she moists the
      ground:
Praised be her beames, the glory of the night,
        Prais'd be her power, by which all powers
        abound.

Prais'd be her Nimphs, with whom she decks the
      woods,
Prais'd be her Knights, in whom true honour lives:
Prais'd be that force, by which she mooves the floods,
        Let that *Diana* shine which all these gives.

In heaven Queene she is among the Spheares,
She Mistresse-like makes all things to be pure:
Eternity in her oft change she beares,
        She beauty is, by her the faire endure.

Time weares her not, she dooth his Chariot guide,
Mortality below her Orbe is plast:
By her the vertue of the starres downe slide.
        In her is vertues perfect Image cast.

    A knowledge pure it is her woorth to know:
    With *Circes* let them dwell, that thinke not so.

The Sheepheards dumpe

LIKE desart Woods, with darksome shades obscured,
Where dreadfull beasts, where hatefull horror raigneth
        Such is my wounded hart, whom sorrow
        paineth.

The Trees are fatall shafts, to death inured,
That cruell love within my hart maintaineth,
        To whet my greefe, when as my sorrow
        waineth.

The ghastly beasts, my thoughts in cares assured,
Which wadge me warre, whilst hart no succour gaineth
        With false suspect, and feare that still re-
        maineth.

The horrors, burning sighs, by cares procured,
Which foorth I send, while weeping eye complaineth,
   To coole the heate the helplesse hart con-
     taineth.

But shafts, but cares, sighs, horrors unrecured,
Were nought esteem'd, if for their paines awarded:
   Your Sheepheards love might be by you
     regarded.
            S. E. D.

wadge] *wage*

The Nimph Dianaes *Song*

Wʜᴇɴ that I poore soule was borne,
I was borne unfortunate:
Presently the Fates had sworne,
To fore-tell my hapless state.

Titan his faire beames did hide,
Phœbe 'clips'd her silver light:
In my birth my Mother died,
Young and faire in heavie plight.

And the Nurse that gave me suck,
Haplesse was in all her life:
And I never had good luck,
Being mayde or married wife.

I lov'd well, and was belov'd,
And forgetting, was forgot:
This a haplesse marriage mov'd,
Greeving that it kills me not.

With the earth would I were wed,
Then in such a grave of woes
Daylie to be buried,
Which no end nor number knowes.

Young my Father married me,
Forc'd by my obedience:
Syrenus, thy faith, and thee
I forgot without offence.

Which contempt I pay so farre,
Never like was paid so much:
Jealousies doo make me warre,
But without a cause of such.

I doo goe with jealous eyes,
To my folds, and to my Sheepe:
And with jealousie I rise,
When the day begins to peepe.

At his table I doo eate,
In his bed with him I lie:
But I take no rest, nor meate,
Without cruell jealousie.

If I aske him what he ayles,
And whereof he jealous is?
In his aunswere then he failes,
Nothing can he say to this.

In his face there is no cheere,
But he ever hangs the head:
In each corner he dooth peere,
And his speech is sad and dead.

Ill the poore soule lives ywis:
That so hardly married is.

Bar. Yong

ywis] *certainly*

104

Rowlands *Madrigall*

FAIRE Love rest thee heere,
Never yet was morne so cleere,
Sweete be not unkinde,
Let me thy favour finde,
    Or else for love I die.
Harke this pretty bubling spring,
How it makes the Meadowes ring,
Love now stand my friend,
Heere let all sorrow end,
    And I will honour thee.
  See where little *Cupid* lyes,
  Looking babies in her eyes.
  Cupid helpe me now,
  Lend to me thy bowe,
    to wound her that wounded me.
  Heere is none to see or tell,
  All our flocks are feeding by,
  This banke with Roses spred,
  Oh it is a dainty bed,
    fit for my Love and me.

Harke the birds in yonder Groave,
How they chaunt unto my Love,
Love be kind to me,
As I have beene to thee,
    for thou hast wonne my hart.
Calme windes blow you faire,
Rock her thou sweete gentle ayre,
O the morne is noone,
The evening comes too soone,
    to part my Love and me.
  The Roses and thy lips doo meete,
  Oh that life were halfe so sweete,
  Who would respect his breath,
  That might die such a death,
    oh that life thus might die.

All the bushes that be neere,
With sweet Nightingales beset,
Hush sweete and be still,
Let them sing their fill,
　　there's none our joyes to let.

Sunne why doo'st thou goe so fast?
Oh why doo'st thou make such hast?
It is too early yet,
So soone from joyes to flit,
　　why art thou so unkind?
See my little Lambkins runne,
Looke on them till I have done,
Hast not on the night,
To rob me of her sight,
　　that live but by her eyes.
　　Alas, sweet Love, we must depart,
　　Harke, my dogge begins to barke,
　　Some bodie's comming neere,
　　They shall not finde us heere,
　　　　for feare of being chid.
　　Take my Garland and my Glove,
　　Weare it for my sake my Love,
　　To morrow on the greene,
　　Thou shalt be our Sheepheards Queene,
　　　　crowned with Roses gay.

Mich. Drayton

Looking babies] in a literal sense *to see one's image in
the pupil of another person's eye　let*] *hinder*

106

Alanius *the Sheepheard, his dolefull Song,* *complayning of* Ismeniaes *crueltie*

No more (ô cruell Nimph,) now hast thou prayed
Enough in thy revenge, proove not thine ire
On him that yeelds, the fault is now appayed
Unto my cost: Now mollifie thy dire
Hardnes, and brest of thine so much obdured:
And now raise up (though lately it hath erred,)
A poore repenting soule, that in the obscured
Darknes of thy oblivion lyes enterred.
    For it falls not in that, that should commend thee:
    That such a Swaine as I may once offend thee.

If that the little Sheepe with speede is flying
From angry Sheepheard (with his words afrayed)
And runneth here and there with fearefull crying,
And with great griefe is from the flock estrayed:
But when it now perceives that none doth follow,
And all alone, so farre estraying, mourneth,
Knowing what danger it is in, with hollow
And fainting bleates, then fearefull it returneth
    Unto the flock, meaning no more to leave it:
    Should it not be a just thing to receave it?

Lift up those eyes (*Ismenia*) which so stately
To view me, thou hast lifted up before me,
That liberty, which was mine owne but lately,
Give me againe, and to the same restore me:
And that mild hart, so full of love and pittie,
Which thou didst yeeld to me, and ever owe me;
Behold (my Nimph) I was not then so wittie
To know that sincere love that thou didst shew me:
    Now wofull man, full well I know and rue it,
    Although it was too late before I knew it.

How could it be (my enemie?) say, tell me,
How thou (in greater fault and errour being
Then ever I was thought) should'st thus repell me?
And with new league and cruell title seeing
They faith so pure and worthy to be changed?
And what is that *Ismenia*, that dooth bind it
To love, whereas the same is most estranged,
And where it is impossible to finde it?
    But pardon me, if heerein I abuse thee:
    Since that the cause thou gav'st me dooth excuse
       me.

But tell me now, what honour hast thou gayned,
Avenging such a fault by thee committed,
And there-unto by thy occasion trayned?
What have I done, that I have not acquitted?
Or what excesse that is not amply payed,
Or suffer more, that I have not endured?
What cruell minde, what angry breast displayed,
With savage hart, to fiercenes so adjured?
    Would not such mortall griefe make milde and
      tender:
    But that, which my fell Sheepheardesse dooth
      render?

Now as I have perceaved well thy reasons,
Which thou hast had, or hast yet to forget me,
The paines, the griefes, the guilts of forced treasons,
That I have done, wherein thou first didst set me:
The passions, and thine eares and eyes refusing
To peare and see me, meaning to undoe me:
Cam'st thou to know, or be but once perusing
Th'unsought occasions, which thou gav'st unto me:
    Thou should'st not have where-with to more tor-
      ment me:
    Nor I to pay the fault my rashnes lent me.

Bar. Yong

Montana *the Sheepheard, his love to* Aminta

I SERVE *Aminta*, whiter then the snowe,
Straighter then Cedar, brighter then the glasse:
More fine in trip, then foote of running Roe,
More pleasant then the field of flowring grasse.
     More gladsome to my withering joyes that fade:
     Then Winters Sunne, or Sommers cooling shade.

Sweeter then swelling Grape of ripest wine,
Softer then feathers of the fairest Swan:
Smoother then Jet, more stately then the Pine,
Fresher then Poplar, smaller then my span.
     Clearer then *Phœbus* fierie pointed beame:
     Or Icie crust of Christalls frozen streame.

Yet is she curster then the Beare by kind,
And harder harted then the aged Oake:
More glib then Oyle, more fickle then the wind,
More stiffe then steele, no sooner bent but broake.
     Loe thus my service is a lasting sore:
     Yet will I serve, although I die therefore.

                              Shep. Tonie

The Sheepheards sorrow for his Phæbes *disdaine*

O H Woods unto your walks my body hies,
To loose the trayterous bonds of tyring Love,
       Where trees, where hearbs, where flowers,
        Their native moisture poures
   From foorth their tender stalkes, to helpe mine
     eyes,
     Yet their united teares may nothing move.

When I behold the faire adorned tree,
Which lightnings force and Winters frost resists,
    Then *Daphnes* ill betide,
    And *Phœbus* lawlesse pride
  Enforce me say, even such my sorrowes be:
For selfe disdaine in *Phœbes* hart consists.

If I behold the flowers by morning teares
Looke lovely sweete: Ah then forlorne I crie
    Sweete showers for *Memnon* shed,
    All flowers by you are fed.
  Whereas my pittious plaint that still appeares,
Yeelds vigor to her scornes, and makes me die.

When I regard the pretty glee-full bird,
With teare-full (yet delightfull) notes complaine:
    I yeeld a terror with my teares,
    And while her musique wounds mine eares,
  Alas say I, when will my notes afford
Such like remorce, who still beweepe my paine?

When I behold upon the leafe-lesse bow
The haplesse bird lament her Loves depart:
    I draw her biding nigh,
    And sitting downe I sigh,
  And sighing say: Alas, that birds avow
A setled faith, yet *Phœbe* scornes my smart.

Thus wearie in my walke, and wofull too,
I spend the day, fore-spent with daily greefe:
    Each object of distresse
    My sorrow dooth expresse
  I doate on that which dooth my hart undoo:
And honour her that scornes to yeeld releefe.

                      Ignoto

Espilus *and* Therion, *their contention in Song for the May-Ladie*

Espilus

TUNE up my voyce, a higher note I yeeld,
To high conceite, the Song must needes be hie:
More high then starres, more firme then flintie field
Are all my thoughts, in which I live and die.
>Sweet soule to whom I vowed am a slave;
>Let not wild woods so great a treasure have.

Therion

The highest note comes oft from basest minde,
As shallow Brookes doo yeeld the greatest sound:
Seeke other thoughts thy life or death to finde,
They starres be falne, plowed is thy flinty ground.
>Sweet soule, let not a wretch that serveth Sheepe,
>Among his Flock so sweete a treasure keepe.

Espilus

Two thousand Sheepe I have as white as milke,
Though not so white as is thy lovely face:
The pasture rich, the wooll as soft as silke,
All this I give, let me possesse thy grace.
>But still take heede, least thou thy selfe submit:
>To one that hath no wealth, and wants his wit.

Therion

Two thousand Deere in wildest woods I have,
Them can I take, but you I cannot hold:
He is not poore who can his freedome save,
Bound but to you, no wealth but you I would.
>But take this beast, if beasts you feare to misse:
>For of his beasts the greatest beast he is.

Both kneeling to her Majestie.

Judge you, to whom all beauties force is lent:

Judge you of love, to whom all love is bent.

> *This Song was sung before the Queenes*
> *most excellent Majestie, in Wansted*
> *Garden: as a contention betweene a*
> *Forrester and a Sheepheard for the*
> *May-Ladie.*
>
> S. Phil. Sidney

Olde Melibeus *Song, courting his Nimph*

Loves Queene long wayting for her true-Love,
    Slaine by a Boare which he had chased,
    Left off her teares, and me embraced,
She kist me sweete, and call'd me new-Love.
        With my silver haire she toyed,
        In my stayed lookes she joyed.
        Boyes (she sayd) breede beauties sorrow:
        Olde men cheere it even and morrow.

My face she nam'd the seate of favour,
    All my defects her tongue defended,
    My shape she prais'd, but most commended
My breath more sweete then Balme in savour.
        Be old man with me delighted,
        Love for love shall be requited.
        With her toyes at last she wone me:
        Now she coyes that hath undone me.

Ignoto

The Sheepheard Sylvanus his Song

MY life (young Sheepheardesse) for thee
       Of needes to death must post:
But yet my greefe must stay with me,
       After my life is lost.

The greevous ill, by Death that cured is,
       Continually hath remedy at hand:
But not that torment that is like to this,
       That in slow time, and Fortunes meanes
         dooth stand.

And if this sorrow cannot be
       Ended with life (at most:)
What then dooth this thing profit me,
       A sorrow wonne or lost?

Yet all is one to me, as now I trie
       a flattering hope, or that that had not been
        yet:
For if to day for want of it I die,
       Next day I doo no lesse for having seene it.

Faine would I die, to end and free
       This greefe, that kills me most:
If that it might be lost with me,
       Or die when life is lost.

Bar. Yong

Coridons Song

A BLITHE and bonny Country-Lasse,
       heigh hoe bonny-Lasse,
Sate sighing on the tender grasse,
       and weeping sayd: will none come woo me?

A smicker Boy, a lither Swaine:
            heigh hoe a smicker Swaine,
That in his love was wanton faine,
            with smiling lookes straite came unto her.

When as the wanton Wench espied,
            heigh hoe when she espied,
The meanes to make her selfe a Bride,
            she simpred smooth like bonnie-bell:
The Swaine that sawe her squint-eyed kinde,
            heigh hoe squint-eyed kinde,
His armes about her body twin'd
            And sayd, Faire Lasse, how fare ye, well?

The Country-Kit sayd, well forsooth,
            heigh hoe well forsooth,
But that I have a longing tooth,
            a longing tooth that makes me crie:
Alas (said he) what garres thy greefe,
            heigh hoe what garres thy greefe?
A wound (quoth she) without releefe,
            I feare a mayde that I shall die.

If that be all, the Sheepheard sayd,
            heigh hoe the Sheepheard sayd,
Ile make thee wive it gentle Mayde,
            and so recure thy maladie:
Heereon they kist with many an oath,
            heigh hoe many an oath,
And fore God *Pan* did plight their troath,
            so to the Church apace they hie.

And God send every pretty peate,
            heigh hoe the pretty peate,
That feares to die of this conceit,
            so kind a friend to helpe at last:

Then Maydes shall never long againe,
        heigh hoe to long againe,
When they finde ease for such a paine.
        thus my Roundelay is past.

Thom. Lodge

smicker] *elegant* or *handsome*   *garres*] *causes*
peate] *a term of endearment to a girl*

The Sheepheards Sonnet

MY fairest *Ganimede* disdaine me not,
      Though sillie Sheepheard I, presume to love
        thee,
      Though my harsh Songs and Sonnets cannot
        moove thee:
Yet to thy beauty is my love no blot:
Apollo, Jove, and many Gods beside
      S'dain'd not the name of Country Sheep-
        heards Swaines,
      Nor want we pleasures, though we take some
        paines.
We live contentedly: A thing call'd pride
Which so corrupts the Court and every place,
      (Each place I meane where learning is
        neglected,
      And yet of late, even learnings selfe's in-
        fected,)
I know not what it meanes in any case.
      We onely (when *Molorchus* gins to peepe,
      Learne for to fold, and to unfold our Sheepe.

Rich. Barnefielde

Selvagia *and* Silvanus, *their Song to* Diana

Sel. I·SEE thee jolly Sheepheard merrie,
    And firme thy faith, and sound as a berrie.
Sil.   Love gave me joy, and Fortune gave it,
       As my desire could wish to have it.

Sel. What didst thou wish, tell me (sweete Lover,)
    Whereby thou might'st such joy recover?
Sil.   To love where love should be inspired:
       Since there's no more to be desired.

Sel. In this great glory, and great gladnes,
    Think'st thou to have no touch of sadnes?
Sil.   Good Fortune gave me not such glorie:
       To mock my Love, or make me sorrie.

Sel. If my firme love I were denying,
    Tell me, with sighs would'st thou be dying?
Sil.   Those words (in jeast) to heare thee speaking:
       For very griefe this hart is breaking.

Sel. Yet would'st thou change, I pre-thee tell me,
    In seeing one that did excell me?
Sil.   O no, for how can I aspire,
       To more, then to mine owne desire?

Sel. Such great affection doo'st thou beare me:
    As by thy words thou seem'st to sweare me?
Sil.   Of thy deserts, to which a debtor
       I am, thou maist demaund this better.

Sel. Sometimes me thinks, that I should sweare it,
    Sometimes me thinks, thou should'st not beare it.
Sil.   Onely in this my hap dooth greeve me,
       And my desire, not to beleeve me.

Sel. Imagine that thou doo'st not love mine,
    But some brave beauty that's above mine.
Sil.   To such a thing (sweete) doo not will me:
    Where faining of the same dooth kill me.

Sel. I see thy firmenesse gentle Lover,
    More then my beauty can discover.
Sil.   And my good fortune to be higher
    Then my desert, but not desire.

Bar. Yong

Montanus *his Madrigall*

IT was a Vallie gawdie greene,
Where *Dian* at the Fount was seene,
    Greene it was,
    And did passe
All other of *Dianaes* bowers,
In the pride of *Floraes* flowers.

A Fount it was that no Sunne sees,
Cirkled in with Cipres trees,
    Set so nie,
    As *Phœbus* eye
Could not doo the Virgins scathe,
To see them naked when they bathe.

She sate there all in white,
Colour fitting her delight,
    Virgins so
    Ought to goe:
For white in Armorie is plaste
To be the colour that is chaste.

Her taffata Cassock you might see,
Tucked up above her knee,
                    Which did show
                    There below
Legges as white as Whales bone,
So white and chast was never none.

Hard by her upon the ground,
Sate her Virgins in a round,
                    Bathing their
                    Golden haire,
And singing all in notes hie:
Fie on *Venus* flattering eye.

Fie on Love, it is a toy,
Cupid witlesse, and a boy,
                    All his fires,
                    And desires,
Are plagues that God sent from on hie:
To pester men with miserie.

As thus the Virgins did disdaine
Lovers joy and Lovers paine,
                    Cupid nie
                    Did espie,
Greeving at *Dianaes* Song,
Slily stole these Maydes among.

His bowe of steele, darts of fire,
He shot amongst them sweete desire,
                    Which straite flies
                    In their eyes.
And at the entraunce made them start,
For it ranne from eye to hart.

Calisto straite supposed *Jove*,
Was faire and frollique for to love.

Dian she,
 Scap'd not free,
For well I wote heere-upon,
She lov'd the Swaine *Endimion.*

Clitia, Phœbus, and *Chloris* eye
Thought none so faire as *Mercurie.*
 Venus thus
 Did discusse
By her Sonne in darts of fire:
None so chast to check desire.

Dian rose with all her Maydes,
Blushing thus at Loves braides,
 With sighs all
 Shew their thrall,
And flinging thence, pronounc'd this saw:
What so strong as Loves sweete law?

Ro. Greene

braides] attacks

Astrophell *to* Stella, *his third Song*

IF *Orpheus* voyce had force to breathe such musiques
  love
Through pores of sencelesse trees, as it could make
  them move:
If stones good measure daunc'd, the *Thebane* walls to
  build
To cadence of the tunes, which *Amphyons* Lyre did
  yeeld:
 More cause a like effect at least-wise bringeth,
 O stones, ô trees, learne hearing *Stella* singeth.

If Love might sweet'n so a boy of Sheepheards broode,
To make a Lyzard dull to tast Loves daintie foode:
If Eagle fierce could so in Grecian Mayde delight,
As his light was her eyes, her death his endlesse night:
    Earth gave that Love, heav'n I trow Love
      defineth,
      O beasts, ô birds, looke, Love, loe, *Stella* shineth.

The birds, stones, and trees feele this, and feeling Love,
And if the trees, nor stones stirre not the same to
           prove:
Nor beasts, nor birds, doo come unto this blessed gaze,
Know, that small Love is quicke, and great Love
           dooth amaze.
    They are amaz'd, but you with reason armed,
    O eyes, ô eares of men, how are you charmed?

S. Phil. Sidney

A Song betweene Syrenus and Sylvanus

Syrenus

Who hath of *Cupids* cates and dainties prayed,
May feede his stomack with them at his pleasure:
If in his drink some ease he hath assayed,
Then let him quench his thirsting without measure:
    And if his weapons pleasant in their manner,
    Let him embrace his standard and his banner.
      For being free from him, and quite exempted:
      Joyfull I am, and proud, and well contented.

Sylvanus

Of *Cupids* daintie cates who hath not prayed,
May be deprived of them at his pleasure:

If wormewood in his drinke he hath assayed,
Let him not quench his thirsting without measure:
  And if his weapons in their cruell manner,
  Let him abjure his standard and his banner:
    For I not free from him, and not exempted,
    Joyfull I am, and proud, and well contented.

Syrenus

Love's so expert in giving many a trouble,
That now I know not why he should be praised:
He is so false, so changing, and so double,
That with great reason he must be dispraised.
  Love in the end is such a jarring passion,
  That none should trust unto his peevish fashion,
    For of all mischiefe he's the onely Maister:
    And to my good a torment and disaster.

Sylvanus

Love's so expert in giving joy, not trouble,
That now I know not but he should be praised:
He is so true, so constant, never double,
That in my minde he should not be dispraised.
  Love in the end is such a pleasing passion,
  That every one may trust unto his fashion.
    For of all good he is the onely Maister:
    And foe unto my harmes, and my disaster.

Syrenus

Not in these sayings to be proov'd a lyer,
He knowes that dooth not love, nor is beloved:
Now nights and dayes I rest, as I desire,
After I had such greefe from me remooved.
  And cannot I be glad, since thus estraunged,
  My selfe from false *Diana* I have chaunged?
    Hence, hence, false Love, I will not entertaine thee:
    Since to thy torments thou doo'st seeke to traine
    me.

Not in these sayings to be proov'd a lyer,
He knowes that loves, and is again beloved:
Now nights and dayes I rest in sweete desire,
After I had such happy fortune prooved.
   And cannot I be glad, since not estraunged,
    My selfe into *Selvagia* I have chaunged
      Come, come, good Love, and I will entertaine
        thee:
       Since to thy sweete content thou seek'st to traine
        me.

Bar. Yong

Ceres *Song in emulation of* Cinthia

SWELL *Ceres* now, for other Gods are shrinking,
    Pomona pineth,
    Fruitlesse her tree:
    Faire *Phœbus* shineth
    Onely on me.
Conceite dooth make me smile whilst I am thinking,
    How every one dooth read my storie,
    How every bough on *Ceres* lowreth,
    Cause heaven plenty on me powreth,
    And they in leaves doo onely glorie,
    All other Gods of power bereaven,
    Ceres onely Queene of heaven.

With roabes and flowers let me be dressed,
    Cinthia that shineth
    Is not so cleare:
    Cinthia declineth
    When I appeare.

122

Yet in this Isle she raignes as blessed,
> And every one at her dooth wonder,
> And in my eares still fond fame whispers
> *Cinthia* shall be *Ceres* Mistres,
> But first my Carre shall rive in sunder.
> Helpe *Phœbus* helpe, my fall is suddaine:
> *Cinthia, Cinthia* must be Soveraigne.

> *This Song was sung before her Majestie,*
> *at Bissam, the Lady* Russels, *in prograce.*
> *The Authors name unknowne to me.*

A Pastorall Ode to an honourable friend

> As to the blooming prime,
> Bleake Winter being fled:
> From compasse of the clime,
> Where Nature lay as dead,
> The Rivers dull'd with time,
> The greene leaves withered,
Fresh *Zephyri* (the Westerne brethren) be:
So th'honour of your favour is to me.
> For as the Plaines revive,
> And put on youthful greene:
> As plants begin to thrive,
> That disattir'd had beene:
> And Arbours now alive,
> In former pompe are seene.
So if my Spring had any flowers before:
Your breathes *Favonius* hath encreast the store.

E. B.

A Nimphs disdaine of Love

HEY downe a downe did *Dian* sing,
    amongst her Virgins sitting:
Then love there is no vainer thing,
    for Maydens most unfitting.
And so think I, with a downe downe derrie.

When women knew no woe,
    but liv'd them-selves to please:
Mens fayning guiles they did not know,
    the ground of their disease.
Unborne was false suspect,
    no thought of jealousie:
From wanton toyes and fond affect,
    the Virgins life was free.
        Hey downe a downe did *Dian* sing, &c.

At length men used charmes,
    to which what Maides gave eare:
Embracing gladly endlesse harmes,
    anone enthralled were.
Thus women welcom'd woe,
    disguis'd in name of love:
A jealous hell, a painted show,
    so shall they finde that prove.

        Hey downe a downe did *Dian* sing,
            amongst her Virgins sitting:
        Then love there is no vainer thing,
            for Maydens most unfitting.
        And so think I, with a downe downe derrie.

Ignoto

Apollos *Love-Song for faire* Daphne

MY hart and tongue were twinnes, at once conceaved
The eldest was my hart, borne dumbe by destinie:
The last my tongue, of all sweet thoughts bereaved,
Yet strung and tun'd, to play harts harmonie.
Both knit in one, and yet a-sunder placed.
What hart would speake, the tongue dooth still dis-
    cover:
What tongue dooth speake, is of the hart embraced,
And both are one, to make a new-found Lover.
New-found, and onely found in Gods and Kings,
Whose words are deedes, but deedes nor words re-
    garded:
Chast thoughts doo mount, and flie with swiftest
    wings,
My love with paine, my paine with losse rewarded.
    Engrave upon this tree *Daphnes* perfection:
    That neither men nor Gods can force affection.

> *This Dittie was sung before her Majestie,
> at the right honourable the Lord Chandos,
> at Sudley Castell, at her last being there
> in prograce. The Author thereof un-
> knowne.*

The Sheepheard Delicius *his Dittie*

NEVER a greater foe did Love disdaine,
    Or trode on grasse so gay,
Nor Nimph greene leaves with whiter hand hath rent,
More golden haire the wind did never blow,
Nor fairer Dame hath bound in white attire,
Or hath in Lawne more gracious features tied,
    Then my sweete Enemie.

Beautie and chastitie one place refraine,
        In her beare equall sway:
Filling the world with wonder and content.
But they doo give me paine and double woe,
Since love and beautie kindled my desire,
And cruell chastitie from me denied
        All sence of jollitie.

There is no Rose, nor Lillie after raine,
        Nor flower in moneth of May,
Nor pleasant meade, nor greene in Sommer sent,
That seeing them, my minde delighteth so,
As that faire flower which all the heavens admire,
Spending my thoughts on her, in whom abide
        All grace and gifts on hie.

Me thinks my heavenly Nimph I see againe
        Her neck and breast display:
Seeing the whitest Ermine to frequent
Some plaine, or flowers that make the fairest show.
O Gods, I never yet beheld her nier,
Or farre, in shade, or Sunne, that satisfied
        I was in passing by.

The Meade, the Mount, the River, Wood, and Plaine,
        With all their brave array,
Yeeld not such sweete, as that faire face that's bent
Sorrowes and joy in each soule to bestow
In equall parts, procur'd by amorous fire:
Beauty and Love in her their force have tried,
        to blind each humane eye.

Each wicked mind and will, which wicked vice dooth
        staine,
        her vertues breake and stay:
All ayres infect by fire are purg'd and spent,
Though of a great foundation they did grow.

O body, that so brave a soule doo'st hire,
And blessed soule, whose vertues ever pried
        above the starrie skie.

Onely for her my life in joyes I traine
        my soule sings many a Lay:
Musing on her, new Seas I doo invent
Of soveraigne joy, wherein with pride I rowe.
The deserts for her sake I doo require,
For without her, the Springs of joy are dried
        and that I doo defie.

Sweete Fate, that to a noble deede doo'st straine,
        and lift my hart to day:
Sealing her there with glorious ornament,
Sweete seale, sweete greefe, and sweetest overthrowe,
Sweete miracle, whose fame cannot expire,
Sweete wound, and golden shaft, that so espied
        such heavenly companie
    Of beauties graces in sweete vertues died,
    As like were never in such yeares descried.

Bar. Yong

Page 126 last line but one ayre *E.H.*, fire in *Diana :*

Amintas *for his* Phillis

AURORA now began to rise againe,
From watry couch, and from old *Tithons* side:
In hope to kisse upon *Acteian* plaine,
Young *Cephalus*, and through the golden glide
On Easterne coast, she cast so great a light,
That *Phœbus* thought it time to make retire
From *Thetis* bower, wherein he spent the night,
To light the world againe with heavenly fire.

No sooner gan his winged Steedes to chase
The Stigian night, mantled with duskie vale:
But poore *Amintas* hasteth him a pace,
In deserts thus, to weepe a wofull tale.
You silent shades, and all that dwell therein,
As birds, or beasts, or wormes that creepe on ground:
Dispose yourselves to teares, while I begin
To rue the greefe of mine eternall wound.

And dolefull ghosts, whose nature flies the light
Come seate your selves with me on ev'ry side:
And while I die for want of my delight,
Lament the woes through fancie me betide.
Phillis is dead, the marke of my desire,
My cause of love, and shipwreck of my joyes,
Phillis is gone that set my hart on fire,
That clad my thoughts with ruinous annoyes.

Phillis is fled, and bides I wote not where,
Phillis (alas) the praise of woman-kinde:
Phillis the Sunne of this our Hemisphere,
Whose beames made me, and many others blinde.
But blinded me (poore Swaine) above the rest,
That like olde *Oedipus* I live in thrall:
Still feele the woorst, and never hope the best,
My mirth in moane, and honey drown'd in gall.

Her faire, but cruell eyes, bewitcht my sight,
Her sweete, but fading speech enthrall'd my thought:
And in her deedes I reaped such delight,
As brought both will and libertie to nought.
Therefore all hope of happines adiew,
Adiew desire the source of all my care:
Despaire tells me, my weale will nere renue,
Till thus my soule dooth passe in *Charons* Crare

Meane time my minde must suffer Fortunes scorne,
My thoughts still wound, like wounds that still are
    greene:
My weakened limbs be layd on beds of thorne,
My life decayes, although my death's fore-seene.
Mine eyes, now eyes no more, but Seas of tears,
Weepe on your fill, to coole my burning brest:
Where love did place desire, twixt hope and feares,
(I say) desire, the Authour of unrest.

And would to God, *Phillis* where ere thou be,
Thy soule did see the sower of mine estate:
My joyes ecclips'd, for onely want of thee
My being with my selfe at foule debate.
My humble vowes, my sufferance of woe,
My sobs and sighs, and ever-watching eyes:
My plaintive teares, my wandring to and fro,
My will to die, my never-ceasing cries.

No doubt but then these sorrowes would perswade,
The doome of death, to cut my vitall twist:
That I with thee amidst th'infernall shade,
And thou with me might sport us as we list.
Oh if thou waite on faire *Proserpines* traine,
And hearest *Orpheus* neere th'Elizian springs:
Entreate thy Queene to free thee thence againe,
And let the *Thracian* guide thee with his strings.

                                    Tho. Watson

Crare] *a small boat*

Faustus *and* Firmius *sing to their Nimph by turnes*

Firmius

OF mine owne selfe I doo complaine,
   And not for loving thee so much,
   But that in deede thy power is such:
That my true love it dooth restraine,
And onely this dooth give me paine,
   For faine I would
   Love her more, if that I could.

Faustus

Thou doo'st deserve who dooth not see,
   To be belov'd a great deale more:
   But yet thou shalt not finde such store
Of love in others as in me:
For all I have I give to thee.
   Yet faine I would
   Love thee more, if that I could.

Firmius

O trie no other Sheepheard Swaine,
   And care not other loves to prove,
   Who though they give thee all their love:
Thou canst not such as mine obtaine.
And wouldst thou have in love more gaine?
   O yet I would
   Love thee more, if that I could.

Faustus

Impossible it is (my friend)
   That any one should me excell
   In love, whose love I will refell,
If that with me he will contend:

My love no equall hath, nor end.
                   And yet I would
                   Love her more, if that I could.

Firmius

Behold how Love my soule hath charm'd,
                   Since first thy beauties I did see,
                   (Which is but little yet to me,)
My freest sences I have harm'd
(To love thee) leaving them unarm'd:
                   And yet I would
                   Love thee more, if that I could.

Faustus

I ever gave, and give thee still
                   Such store of love, as Love hath lent me:
                   And therefore well thou maist content
                       thee,
That Love dooth so enrich my fill:
But now behold my cheefest will,
                   That faine I would
                   Love thee more, if that I could.

                                          Bar. Yong

refell] *refute*

Sireno *a Sheepheard, having a lock of his faire Nimphs haire, wrapt about with greene silke, mournes thus in a Love-Dittie*

> WHAT changes heere, ô haire,
> I see since I saw you?
> How ill fits you this greene to weare,
> For hope the colour due?

131

In deede I well did hope,
Though hope were mixt with feare:
No other Sheepheard should have scope
Once to approach this heare.

Ah haire, how many dayes,
My *Dian* made me show,
With thousand prettie childish playes,
If I ware you or no?
Alas, how oft with teares,
(Oh teares of guilefull brest:)
She seemed full of jealous feares,
Whereat I did but jest?

Tell me ô haire of gold,
If I then faultie be:
That trust those killing eyes I would,
Since they did warrant me?
Have you not seene her moode,
What streames of teares she spent:
Till that I sware my faith so stoode,
As her words had it bent?

Who hath such beautie seene,
In one that changeth so?
Or where one loves, so constant beene,
Who ever saw such woe?
Ah haires, you are not greev'd,
To come from whence you be:
Seeing how once you saw I liv'd,
To see me as you see.

On sandie banke of late,
I saw this woman sit:
Where, *Sooner die then change my state,*
She with her finger writ.

Thus my beleefe was stay'd,
Behold Loves mighty hand,
On things, were by a woman say'd,
And written in the sand.

Translated by S. Phil. Sidney, *out of*
Diana *of* Montmaior

A Song betweene Taurisius *and* Diana, *aunswering verse for verse*

Taurisius. THE cause why that thou doo'st denie
　　　　To looke on me, sweete foe impart?
Diana. Because that dooth not please the eye,
　　　　Which dooth offend and greeve the
　　　　　　hart.
Taurisius. What woman is, or ever was,
　　　　That when she looketh, could be
　　　　　　mov'd?
Diana. She that resolves her life to passe,
　　　　Neyther to love, nor to be lov'd.
Taurisius. There is no hart so fierce and hard
　　　　That can so much torment a soule:
Diana. Nor Sheepheard of so small regard,
　　　　That reason will so much controule.
Taurisius. How falls it out Love dooth not kill
　　　　Thy crueltie with some remorce?
Diana. Because that Love is but a will,
　　　　And free-will dooth admit no force.
Taurisius. Behold what reason now thou hast,
　　　　To remedie my loving smart:
Diana. The very same bindes me as fast,
　　　　To keepe such daunger from my hart.
Taurisius. Why doo'st thou thus torment my minde,
　　　　And to what end thy beautie keepe?

Diana. Because thou call'st me still unkinde,
             And pittilesse when thou doo'st weepe.
Taurisius. Is it because thy crueltie
             In killing me doth never end?
Diana. Nay, for because I meane thereby,
             My hart from sorrow to defend.
Taurisius. Be bold; so foule I am no way
             As thou doo'st think, faire Sheep-
             heardesse:
Diana. With this content thee, that I say,
             That I beleeve the same no lesse.
Taurisius. What, after giving me such store
             Of passions, doo'st thou mock me too?
Diana. If aunsweres thou wilt any more.
             Goe seeke them without more adoo.

Bar. Yong

Another Song before her Majestie at Oxford, sung by a comely Sheepheard, attended on by sundrie other Sheepheards and Nimphs

HEARBS, words, and stones, all maladies have cured,
      Hearbs, words, and stones, I used when I loved:
Hearbs smells, words winde, stones hardnes have
           procured,
      By stones, nor words, nor hearbs her mind was
        moved.
I ask'd the cause: this was a womans reason,
      Mongst hearbs are weedes, and thereby are
        refused:
Deceite as well as trueth speakes words in season,
      False stones by foiles have many one abused.

I sigh'd, and then she sayd, my fancie smoaked,
    I gaz'd, she sayd, my lookes were follies
      glauncing:
I sounded dead, she sayd, my love was choaked,
    I started up, she sayd, my thoughts were
      dauncing.
      Oh sacred Love, if thou have any Godhead:
      Teach other rules to winne a maydenhead.

Anonimus

The Sheepheards Song: a Caroll or Himne for Christmas

      Sweete Musique, sweeter farre
      Then any Song is sweete:
      Sweete Musique heavenly rare,
      Mine eares (ô peeres) dooth greete.
You gentle flocks, whose fleeces pearl'd with dewe,
Resemble heaven, whom golden drops make bright:
Listen, ô listen, now, ô not to you
Our pipes make sport to shorten wearie night,
      But voyces most divine,
      Make blisfull Harmonie:
      Voyces that seeme to shine,
      For what else cleares the skie?
    Tunes can we heare, but not the Singers see:
    The tunes divine, and so the Singers be.

      Loe how the firmament,
      Within an azure fold:
      The flock of starres hath pent,
      That we might them behold.
Yet from their beames proceedeth not this light,
Nor can their Christalls such reflection give:

What then dooth make the Element so bright?
The heavens are come downe upon earth to live.
      But harken to the Song,
      Glorie to glories King:
      And peace all men among,
      These Queristers doo sing.
  Angels they are, as also (Sheepheards) hee,
Whom in our feare we doo admire to see.

      Let not amazement blinde
      Your soules (said he) annoy:
      To you and all mankinde,
      My message bringeth joy.
For loe the worlds great Sheepheard now is borne
A blessed Babe, an Infant full of power:
After long night, up-risen is the morne,
Renowning *Bethlem* in the Saviour.
      Sprung is the perfect day,
      By Prophets seen a farre:
      Sprung is the mirthfull May,
      Which Winter cannot marre,
  In *Davids* Cittie dooth this Sunne appeare:
Clouded in flesh, yet Sheepheards sit we here.

                  E. B.

Arsileus *his Caroll, for joy of the new mari-age, betweene* Syrenus *and* Diana

LET now each Meade with flowers be depainted,
  Of sundry colours sweetest odours glowing:
Roses yeeld foorth your smells so finely tainted,
  Calme winds the greene leaves moove with gentle
      blowing,

The Christall Rivers flowing
With waters be encreased:
And since each one from sorrow now hath
    ceased,
From mournfull plaints and sadnes.
Ring foorth faire Nimphs your joyfull Songs
    for gladnes.

Let Springs and Meades all kinde of sorrow banish,
    And mournfull harts the teares that they are
        bleeding:
Let gloomie cloudes with shining morning vanish,
    Let every bird rejoyce that now is breeding.
        And since by new proceeding,
        With mariage now obtained,
        A great content by great contempt is gained,
        And you devoyd of sadnes,
        Ring foorth faire Nimphs your joyfull Songs
        for gladnes.

Who can make us to change our firme desires,
    And soule to leave her strong determination,
And make us freeze in Ice, and melt in fires,
    And nicest harts to love with emulation,
        Who rids us from vexation,
        And all our minds commaundeth?
        But great *Felicia*, that his might with-
        standeth,
        That fill'd our harts with sadnes,
        Ring foorth faire Nimphs your joyfull Songs
        for gladnes.

Your fields with their distilling favours cumber
    (Bridegroome and happy Bride) each heavenly
        power
Your flocks, with double Lambs encreas'd in number
    May never tast unsavorie grasse and sower.

The Winters frost and shower
Your Kids (your pretie pleasure)
May never hurt, and blest with so much
   treasure,
To drive away all sadnes:
Ring foorth faire Nimphs your joyfull Songs
   for gladnes.

Of that sweete joy delight you with such measure,
   Betweene you both faire issue to engender:
Longer then *Nestor* may you live in pleasure,
   The Gods to you such sweete content surrender,
     That may make mild and tender,
     The beasts in every mountaine,
     And glad the fields, and woods, and every
      Fountaine,
     Abjuring former sadnes,
     Ring foorth faire Nimphs your joyfull Songs
      for gladnes.

Let amorous birds with sweetest notes delight you,
   Let gentle winds refresh you with their blowing:
Let fields and Forrests with their good requite you,
   And *Flora* decke the ground where you are going.
     Roses and Violets strowing,
     The Jasmine and the Gilliflower,
     With many more, and never in your bower,
     To tast of houshold sadnes:
     Ring foorth faire Nimphs your joyfull Songs
      for gladnes.

Concord and peace hold you for aye contented,
   And in your joyfull state live you so quiet:
That with the plague of jealousie tormented
   You may not be, nor fed with Fortunes diet.
     And that your names may flie yet,
     To hills unknowne with glorie.

But now because my breast so hoarce, and
    sorrie
It faints, may rest from singing:
End Nimphs your songs, that in the clouds
    are ringing.

Bar. Yong

Philistus *farewell to false* Clorinda

CLORINDA false adiew, thy love torments me:
Let *Thirsis* have thy hart, since he contents thee.
      Oh greefe and bitter anguish,
        For thee I languish,
      Faine I (alas) would hide it,
        Oh, but who can abide it.
      I can, I cannot I abide it?
      Adiew, adiew then,
        Farewell,
      Leave my death now desiring:
      For thou hast thy requiring.
      Thus spake *Philistus*, on his hooke relying:
        And sweetly fell a dying.

Out of M. Morleyes Madrigalls

Rosalindes *Madrigall*

LOVE in my bosome like a Bee,
    dooth suck his sweete:
Now with his wings he playes with me,
    now with his feete.

139

Within mine eyes he makes his nest,
His bed amidst my tender brest,
My kisses are his daily feast,
And yet he robs me of my rest.
      Ah wanton will ye?

And if I sleepe, then pierceth he,
      with prettie slight:
And makes his pillow of my knee,
      the live-long night.
Strike I my Lute, he tunes the string.
He musique playes if I but sing,
He lends me every lovely thing,
Yet cruell he my hart dooth sting.
      Whist wanton, still ye.

Else I with Roses every day
      will whip ye hence:
And binde ye when ye long to play,
      for your offence.
Ile shut mine eyes to keepe ye in,
Ile make you fast it for your sinne,
Ile count your power not woorth a pin.
Alas, what heereby shall I winne
      If he gaine-say me?

What if I beate the wanton boy
      with many a rod?
He will repay me with annoy,
      because a God.
Then sit thou safely on my knee,
And let thy bower my bosome be:
Lurke in mine eyes, I like of thee.
O *Cupid*, so thou pitty me,
      Spare not, but play thee.

Thom. Lodge

A Dialogue Song betweene Sylvanus
and Arsilius

Syl. SHEEPHEARD, why doo'st thou hold thy peace?
      Sing, and thy joy to us report:
Arsil.   My joy good (Sheepheard) should be lesse,
      If it were told in any sort.
Syl. Though such great favours thou doo'st winne,
      Yet daigne thereof to tell some part:
Arsil.   The hardest thing is to begin,
      In enterprizes of such Art.
Syl. Come make an end, no cause omit,
      Of all the joyes that thou art in:
Arsil.   How should I make an end of it,
      That am not able to begin?
Syl. It is not just, we should consent,
      That thou should'st not thy joyes recite:
Arsil.   The soule that felt the punishment,
      Dooth onely feele this great delight.
Syl. That joy is small, and nothing fine,
      That is not told abroade to manie:
Arsil.   If it be such a joy as mine,
      It can be never told to anie.
Syl. How can this hart of thine containe
      A joy, that is of such great force?
Arsil.   I have it, where I did retaine
      My passions of so great remorce.
Syl. So great and rare a joy is this,
      No man is able to with-hold:
Arsil.   But greater that a pleasure is,
      The lesse it may with words be told.
Syl. Yet have I heard thee heeretofore,
      Thy joyes in open Songs report:
Arsil.   I said, I had of joy some store,
      But not how much, nor in what sort.
Syl. Yet when a joy is in excesse,
      It selfe it will oft-times unfold:

Arsil.   Nay, such a joy would be the lesse,
            If but a word thereof were told.

Bar. Yong

Montanus *Sonnet*

WHEN the dogge
Full of rage
    With his irefull eyes
    Frownes amidst the skies:
The Sheepheard to asswage
The furie of the heate,
Him selfe dooth safely seate
    By a Fount
    Full of faire,
    Where a gentle breath
    Mounting from beneath,
       tempereth the ayre.
There his flocks
Drinke their fill,
    And with ease repose,
    While sweet sleepe doth close
Eyes from toyling ill,
But I burne,
Without rest,
    No defensive power
    Shields from *Phœbus* lower,
       sorrow is my best.
Gentle Love
Lower no more,
    If thou wilt invade
    In the secret shade,
Labour not so sore,
    I my selfe

142

And my flocks,
>   They their Love to please,
>   I my selfe to ease,
Both leave the shadie Oakes,
>   Content to burne in fire,
>   Sith Love dooth so desire.

S. E. D.

The Nymph Selvagia *her Song*

SHEEPHEARD, who can passe such wrong,
>   And a life in woes so deepe?
Which to live is to too long,
>   As it is too short to weepe.

Greevous sighs in vaine I wast,
>   Leesing my affiance, and
I perceave my hope at last
>   with a candle in the hand.

What time then to hope among
>   bitter hopes, that never sleepe?
When this life is to too long,
>   as it is too short to weepe.

This greefe which I feele so rife,
>   (wretch) I doo deserve as hire:
Since I came to put my life
>   in the hands of my desire.

Then cease not my complaints so strong,
>   for (though life her course dooth keepe:)
It is not to live so long,
>   as it is too short to weepe.

Bar. Yong

The Heard-mans happie life

WHAT pleasure have great Princes,
　　more daintie to their choice,
Then Heardmen wilde, who carelesse,
　　in quiet life rejoyce?
　　And Fortunes Fate not fearing,
　　Sing sweet in Sommer morning.

Their dealings plaine and rightfull
　　are voide of all deceite:
They never know how spightfull,
　　it is to kneele and waite;
　　On favourite presumptuous,
　　Whose pride is vaine and sumptuous.

All day theyr flocks each tendeth,
　　at night they take their rest:
More quiet then who sendeth
　　his ship into the East;
　　Where gold and pearle are plentie,
　　But getting very daintie.

For Lawyers and their pleading,
　　they'steeme it not a straw:
They thinke that honest meaning,
　　is of it selfe a law;
　　Where conscience judgeth plainely,
　　They spend no money vainely.

Oh happy who thus liveth,
　　not caring much for gold:
With cloathing which suffiseth,
　　to keepe him from the cold.
　　Though poore and plaine his diet:
　　Yet merrie it is and quiet.

Out of M. Birds *set Songs*

Cinthia *the Nimph, her Song to faire* Polydora

NEERE to the River banks, with greene
And pleasant trees on every side,
Where freest minds would most have beene,
That never felt brave *Cupids* pride,
      To passe the day and tedious howers:
      Amongst those painted meades and
        flowers.

A certaine Sheepheard full of woe,
Syrenus call'd, his flocks did feede:
Not sorrowfull in outward show,
But troubled with such greefe indeede,
      As cruell Love is wont t'impart
      Unto a painefull loving hart.

This Sheepheard every day did die,
For love he to *Diana* bare:
A Sheepheardesse so fine perdie,
So lively, young, and passing faire,
      Excelling more in beauties feature:
      Then any other humane creature.

Who had not any thing, of all
She had, but was extreame in her,
For meanely wise none might her call,
Nor meanely faire, for he did erre
      If so he did: but should devise
      Her name of passing faire and wise.

Favours on him she did bestow,
Which if she had not, then be sure
He might have suffered all that woe
Which afterward he did endure
      When he was gone, with lesser paine:
      And at his comming home againe.

For when indeede the hart is free
From suffering paine or torments smart:
If wisdome dooth not over-see
And beareth not the greatest part;
   The smallest greefe and care of minde:
   Dooth make it captive to their kinde.

Neere to a River swift and great,
That famous *Ezla* had to name:
The carefull Sheepheard did repeate
The feares he had by absence blame,
   Which he suspect where he did keepe:
   And feede his gentle Lambs and Sheepe.

And now sometimes he did behold
His Sheepheardesse, that there about
Was on the mountaines of that old
And auncient *Leon*, seeking out
   From place to place the pastures best:
   Her Lambs to feede, her selfe to rest.

And sometime musing, as he lay,
When on those hills she was not seene:
Was thinking of that happie day,
When *Cupid* gave him such a Queene
   Of beautie, and such cause of joy:
   Wherein his minde he did imploy.

Yet sayd (poore man) when he did see
Him selfe so sunke in sorrowes pit:
The good that Love hath given me,
I onely doo imagine it,
   Because this neerest harme and trouble:
   Heereafter I should suffer double.

The Sunne for that it did decline,
The carelesse man did not offend
With fierie beames, which scarce did shine,
But that which did of love depend,
        And in his hart did kindle fire:
        Of greater flames and hote desire.

Him did his passions all invite,
The greene leaves blowne with gentle winde:
Christaline streames with their delight,
And Nightingales were not behinde,
        To helpe him in his loving verse:
        Which to himselfe he did rehearse.

Bar. Yong

The Sheepheard to the flowers

SWEET Violets (Loves Paradise) that spread
Your gracious odours, which you couched beare
        Within your palie faces.
Upon the gentle wing of some calme-breathing-
        winde
        That playes amidst the Plaine,
        If by the favour of propitious starres you
        gaine
Such grace as in my Ladies bosome place to finde:
        Be proude to touch those places.
And when her warmth your moysture foorth dooth
        weare,
Whereby her daintie parts are sweetly fed:
        Your honours of the flowrie Meades I
        pray
        You prettie daughters of the earth and
        Sunne:

With mild and seemely breathing straite
  display
My bitter sighs, that have my hart un-
  done.

Vermillion Roses, that with new dayes rise
Display your crimson folds fresh looking faire,
  Whose radiant bright, disgraces
The rich adorned rayes of roseate rising morne,
  Ah if her Virgins hand
    Doo pluck your pure, ere *Phœbus* view
      the land,
And paile your gracious pompe in lovely Natures
  scorne.
    If chaunce my Mistres traces
Fast by your flowers to take the Sommers ayre:
Then wofull blushing tempt her glorious eyes,
    To spread their teares, *Adonis* death re-
      porting,
    And tell Loves torments, sorrowing for
      her friend:
    Whose drops of blood within your
      leaves consorting,
    Report faire *Venus* moanes to have no
      end.
Then may remorce, in pittying of my smart:
Drie up my teares, and dwell within her hart.

                                    Ignoto

The Sheepheard Arsilius, his Song to his Rebeck

Now Love and Fortune turne to me againe,
   And now each one enforceth and assures
   A hope, that was dismayed, dead, and
    vaine:
And from the harbour of mishaps assures
   A hart that is consum'd in burning fire,
   With unexpected gladnes, that adjures
My soule to lay a-side her mourning tire,
   And sences to prepare a place for joy,
   Care in oblivion endlesse shall expire.
For every greefe of that extreame annoy,
   Which when my torment raign'd, my soule
    (alas)
   Did feele, the which long absence did
    destroy,
Fortune so well appayes, that never was
   So great the torment of my passed ill:
   As is the joy of this same good I passe.
Returne my hart, sursaulted with the fill
   Of thousand great unrests, and thousand
    feares:
   Enjoy thy good estate, if that thou will,
And wearied eyes, leave off your burning teares,
   For soone you shall behold her with
    delight,
   For whom my spoiles with glorie *Cupid*
    beares.
Sences which seeke my starre so cleare and bright,
   By making heere and there your thoughts
    estray:
   Tell me, what will you feele before her
    sight?

Hence solitarinesse, torments away,
>> Felt for her sake, and wearied members
>>> cast
>> Of all your paine, redeem'd this happie
>>> day.
O stay not time, but passe with speedie hast,
>> And Fortune hinder not her comming now
>> O God, betides me yet this greefe at last?
Come my sweete Sheepheardesse, the life which thou
>> (Perhaps) didst thinke was ended long
>>> agoe,
>> At thy commaund is readie still to bow.
Comes not my Sheepheardesse desired so?
>> O God, what if she's lost, or if she stray
>> Within this wood, where trees so thick
>>> doo grow?
Or if this Nimph that lately went away,
>> Perhaps forgot to goe and seeke her out:
>> No, no, in (her) oblivion never lay.
Thou onely art my Sheepheardesse, about
>> Whose thoughts my soule shall find her joy
>>> and rest:
>> Why comm'st not then to assure it from
>>> doubt?
O seest thou not the Sunne passe to the West?
>> And if it passe, and I behold thee not:
>> Then I my wonted torments will request
>> And thou shalt waile my hard and heavie
>>> lot.

Bar. Yong

Rebeck] *a stringed instrument played with a bow*
sursaulted] *attacked suddenly*

Another of Astrophell *to his* Stella

In a Groave most rich of shade,
Where birds wanton musique made;
May, then young, his pyed weedes showing,
New perfum'd, with flowers fresh growing.
Astrophell with *Stella* sweete,
Did for mutuall comfort meete,
Both within them-selves oppressed,
But each in the other blessed.

    Him great harmes had taught much care,
Her faire necke a foule yoake bare:
But her sight his cares did banish,
In his sight her yoake did vanish.
Wept they had, alas the while,
But now teares them-selves did smile.
While their eyes by Love directed,
Enterchangeably reflected.

    Sigh they did, but now betwixt,
Sighs of woes, were glad sighs mixt,
With armes crost, yet testifying
Restlesse rest, and living dying.
Their eares hungry of each word,
Which the deare tongue would afford,
But their tongues restrain'd from walking,
Till their harts had ended talking.

    But when their tongues could not speake,
Love it selfe did silence breake,
Love did set his lips a-sunder,
Thus to speake in love and wonder.
Stella, Soveraigne of my joy,
Faire triumpher of annoy,
Stella, starre of heavenly fire,
Stella, Loadstarre of desire.

    Stella, in whose shining eyes,
Are the lights of *Cupids* skies,
Whose beames where they once are darted,
Love there-with is straite imparted.

Stella, whose voyce when it speakes,
Sences all a-sunder breakes.
Stella, whose voyce when it singeth,
Angels to acquaintance bringeth.

    Stella, in whose body is
Writ each Character of blisse,
Whose face all, all beauty passeth,
Save thy minde, which it surpasseth.
Graunt, ô graunt: but speech alas
Failes me, fearing on to passe.
Graunt, ô me, what am I saying?
But no fault there is in praying.

      Graunt (ô deere) on knees I pray,
(Knees on ground he then did stay)
That not I, but since I love you,
Time and place for me may moove you.
Never season was more fit,
Never roome more apt for it.
Smiling ayre alowes my reason.
The birds sing, now use the season.

      This small winde, which so sweete is,
See how it the leaves dooth kisse,
Each tree in his best attyring
Sence of love to love inspiring.
Love makes earth the water drinke,
Love to earth makes water sinke:
And if dumbe things be so wittie,
Shall a heavenly grace want pittie?

      There his hands in their speech, faine
Would have made tongues language plaine.
But her hands, his hands repelling:
Gave repulse, all grace excelling.
Then she spake; her speech was such,
As not eares, but hart did touch:
While such wise she love denied,
As yet love she signified.

    Astrophell, she said, my Love,
Cease in these effects to prove.

Now be still, yet still beleeve me,
Thy greefe more then death dooth greeve me.
If that any thought in me,
Can tast comfort but of thee,
Let me feede with hellish anguish,
Joylesse, helplesse, endlesse languish.
    If those eyes you praised, be
Halfe so deere as you to me:
Let me home returne starke blinded
Of those eyes, and blinder minded.
If to secret of my hart
I doo any wish impart:
Where thou art not formost placed;
Be both wish and I defaced.
    If more may be said, I say
All my blisse on thee I lay.
If thou love, my love content thee,
For all love, all faith is meant thee.
Trust me, while I thee denie,
In my selfe the smart I trie.
Tirant, honour dooth thus use thee,
Stellaes selfe might not refuse thee.
    Therefore (deere) this no more move,
Least, though I leave not thy love,
Which too deepe in me is framed:
I should blush when thou art named.
There-with-all, away she went,
Leaving him to passion rent:
With what she had done and spoken,
That there-with my Song is broken.

S. Phil. Sidney

Syrenus *his Song to* Dianaes *Flocks*

PASSED contents,
Oh what meane ye?
Forsake me now, and doo not wearie me.
Wilt thou heare me ô memorie,
My pleasant dayes, and nights againe,
I have appai'd with seaven-fold paine.
Thou hast no more to aske me why,
For when I went, they all did die
As thou doo'st see:
O leave me then, and doo not wearie me.

Greene field, and shadowed valley, where
Sometime my chiefest pleasure was,
Behold what I did after passe.
Then let me rest, and if I beare
Not with good cause continuall feare:
Now doo you see,
O leave me then, and doo not trouble me.

I saw a hart changed of late,
And wearied to assure mine:
Then I was forced to recure mine
By good occasion, time, and fate,
My thoughts that now such passions hate
O what meane ye?
Forsake me now, and doo not wearie me.
You Lambs and Sheepe that in these Layes,
Did sometime follow me so glad:
The merrie houres, and the sad
Are passed now, with all those dayes.
Make not such mirth and wunted playes
As once did ye.
For now no more, you have deceaved me.

If that to trouble me you come,
Or come to comfort me in deede:
I have no ill for comforts neede.
But if to kill me: Then (in some)
Now my joyes are dead and dombe,
      Full well may ye
      Kill me, and you shall make an end of me.

Bar. Yong

To Amarillis

THOUGH *Amarillis* daunce in greene,
      Like Faierie Queene,
      And sing full cleere,
      With smiling cheere.
Yet since her eyes make hart so sore,
      hey hoe, chill love no more.

My Sheepe are lost for want of foode
      And I so wood
      That all the day:
I sit and watch a Heard-mayde gay
Who laughs to see me sigh so sore:
      hey hoe, chill love no more.

Her loving lookes, her beautie bright,
      Is such delight,
      That all in vaine:
I love to like, and loose my gaine,
For her that thanks me not therefore,
      hey hoe, chill love no more.

Ah wanton eyes, my friendly foes,
      And cause of woes,
        Your sweet desire
Breedes flames of ice, and freeze in fire.
You scorne to see me weepe so sore:
        hey hoe, chill love no more.

Love ye who list, I force him not,
      Sith God it wot
        The more I waile:
The lesse my sighs and teares prevaile.
What shall I doo, but say therefore,
        hey hoe, chill love no more?

Out of M. Birds *set Songs*

wood] *mad or furious with rage*

Cardenia *the Nimph, to her false*
Sheepheard Faustus

FAUSTUS, if thou wilt reade from me
    These fewe and simple lines,
By them most clearly thou shalt see,
How little should accounted be
    Thy faigned words and signes.
For noting well thy deedes unkinde,
    Sheepheard, thou must not scan:
That ever it came to my minde,
To praise thy faith like to the winde,
    Or for a constant man.

For this in thee shall so be found,
    As smoake blowne in the aire:

156

Or like Quick-silver turning round,
Or as a house built on the ground
    Of sands that doo impaire.
To firmnesse thou art contrarie,
    More slipp'rie then the Eele:
Changing as Weather-cocke on hie,
Or the Camelion on the die,
    Or Fortunes turning wheele.

Who would beleeve thou wert so free,
    To blaze me thus each houre?
My Sheepheardesse, thou liv'st in me,
My soule dooth onely dwell in thee,
    And every vitall power.
Pale *Atropos* my vitall string
    Shall cut, and life offend:
The streames shall first turne to their spring,
The world shall end, and everything,
    Before my love shall end.

This love that thou didst promise me,
    Sheepheard, where is it found?
The word and faith I had of thee,
O tell me now, where may they be,
    Or where may they resound?
Too soone thou did'st the tytle gaine
    Of giver of vaine words:
Too soone my love thou did'st obtaine,
Too soone thou lov'dst *Diana* in vaine,
    That nought but scornes affords.

But one thing now I will thee tell,
    That much thy pacience mooves:
That though *Diana* dooth excell
In beautie, yet she keepes not well
    Her faith, nor loyall prooves.
Thou then hast chosen, each one saith,
    Thine equall, and a shrow:

For if thou hast undone thy faith,
Her love and Lover she betrayeth,
   So like to like may goe.

If now this Sonnet which I send
   Will anger thee: Before
Remember *Faustus* (yet my friend,)
That if these speeches doo offend,
   Thy deedes doo hurt me more.
Thus let each one of us amend,
   Thou deedes, I words so spent:
For I confesse I blame my pen,
Doo thou as much, so in the end,
   Thy deedes thou do repent.

Bar. Yong

shrow] obsolete form of *shrew*

Of Phillida

As I beheld, I saw a Heardman wilde,
   with his sheep-hooke a picture fine deface:
Which he sometime his fancie to beguile,
   had carv'd on bark of Beech in secret place.
And with despight of most afflicted minde,
   through deepe dispaire of hart, for love dismaid
He pull'd even from the tree the carved rinde,
   and weeping sore, these wofull words he said.
Ah *Phillida*, would God thy picture faire,
   I could as lightly blot out of my brest:
Then should I not thus rage in deepe dispaire,
   and teare the thing sometime I liked best.
     But all in vaine, it booteth not God wot:
     What printed is in hart, on tree to blot.

Out of M. Birds *set Songs*

Melisea *her Song, in scorne of her Sheep-heard* Narcissus

YOUNG Sheepheard turne a-side, and move
    Me not to follow thee:
For I will neither kill with love,
    Nor love shall not kill me.

Since I will live, and never show,
    Then die not, for my love I will not give
For I will never have thee love me so,
    As I doo meane to hate thee while I live.

That since the lover so dooth prove,
    His death, as thou doo'st see:
Be bold I will not kill with love,
    Nor love shall not kill me.

Bar. Yong

His aunswere to the Nimphs Song

IF to be lov'd it thee offend,
    I cannot choose but love thee still:
And so thy greefe shall have no end,
    Whiles that my life maintaines my will.

O let me yet with greefe complaine,
    since such a torment I endure:
Or else fulfill thy great disdaine,
    to end my life with death most sure.
For as no credite thou wilt lend,
    and as my love offends thee still:
So shall thy sorrowes have no end,
    whiles that my life maintaines my will.

If that by knowing thee, I could
    leave off to love thee as I doo:
Not to offend thee, then I would
    leave off to like and love thee too.
But since all love to thee dooth tend,
    and I of force must love thee still:
Thy greefe shall never have an end,
    whiles that my life maintaines my will.

Bar. Yong

Her present aunswere againe to him

ME thinks thou tak'st the worser way,
    (Enamoured Sheepheard) and in vaine
That thou wilt seeke thine own decay,
    To love her, that dooth thee disdaine.

For thine owne selfe, thy wofull hart
    Keepe still, else art thou much to blame:
For she to whom thou gav'st each part
    Of it, disdaines to take the same.

Follow not her that makes a play,
    And jest of all thy greefe and paines:
And seeke not (Sheepheard) thy decay.
    To love her that thy love disdaines.

Bar. Yong

thy greefe] the reading in *Diana; E.H.* has *the greefe*

160

His last replie

SINCE thou to me wert so unkinde,
    My selfe, I never loved, for
I could not love him in my minde,
    Whom thou (faire Mistresse) doo'st abhorre.

If viewing thee, I sawe thee not,
    And seeing thee, I could not love thee:
Dying, I should not live (God wot)
    Nor living, should to anger moove thee.

But it is well that I doo finde
    My life so full of torments, for
All kinde of ills doo fit his minde
    Whom thou (faire Mistress) doo'st abhorre.

In thy oblivion buried now
    My death I have before mine eyes:
And heere to hate my selfe I vow,
    As (cruell) thou doo'st me despise.

Contented ever thou didst finde
    Me with thy scornes, though never (for
To say the trueth) I joyed in minde,
    After thou didst my love abhorre.

Bar. Yong

Philon *the Sheepheard, his Song*

WHILE that the Sunne with his beames hot,
Scorched the fruites in vale and mountaine:
Philon the Sheepheard late forgot,
Sitting besides a Christall Fountaine:
        In shaddow of a greene Oake tree,
        Upon his Pipe this Song plaid he.
  Adiew Love, adiew Love, untrue Love,
  Untrue Love, untrue Love, adiew Love:
  Your minde is light, soone lost for new love.

So long as I was in your sight,
I was as your hart, your soule, and treasure:
And evermore you sob'd and sigh'd,
Burning in flames beyond all measure.
        Three dayes endured your love to me:
        And it was lost in other three.
  Adiew Love, adiew Love, untrue Love. &c.

Another Sheepheard you did see,
To whom your hart was soone enchained:
Full soone your love was leapt from me,
Full soone my place he had obtained.
        Soone came a third, your love to win:
        And we were out, and he was in.
  Adiew Love. &c.

Sure you have made me passing glad,
That you your minde so soone removed:
Before that I the leysure had,
To choose you for my best beloved.
        For all my love was past and done:
        Two dayes before it was begun.
  Adiew Love. &c.

Out of M. Birds *set Songs*

162

Lycoris *the Nimph, her sad Song*

IN dewe of Roses, steeping her lovely cheekes,
      Lycoris thus sate weeping.
Ah *Dorus* false, that hast my hart bereft me,
And now unkinde hast left me.
      Heare alas, oh heare me,
        Aye me, aye me,
      Cannot my beautie moove thee?
      Pitty, yet pitty me,
        Because I love thee.
Aye me, thou scorn'st the more I pray thee:
And this thou doo'st, and all to slay me.
      Why doo then,
      Kill me, and vaunt thee:
        Yet my Ghoast
      Still shall haunt thee.

Out of M. Morleyes *Madrigalls*

To his Flocks

BURST foorth my teares, assist my forward greefe
And shew what paine imperious love provokes:
Kinde tender Lambs, lament Loves scant releefe,
And pine, since pensive care my freedome yoakes,
      Oh pine, to see me pine, my tender Flocks.

Sad pyning care, that never may have peace,
At Beauties gate, in hope of pittie knocks:
But mercie sleepes, while deepe disdaines encrease,
And Beautie hope in her faire bosome yoakes:
      Oh greeve to heare my greefe, my tender
      Flocks:

163

Like to the windes my sighs have winged beene,
Yet are my sighs and sutes repaide with mocks:
I pleade, yet she repineth at my teene,
O ruthless rigour, harder then the Rocks,
      That both the Sheepheard kills, and his
        poore Flocks.

teene] *injury*

To his Love

COME away, come sweet Love,
The golden morning breakes:
All the earth, all the ayre,
Of love and pleasure speakes.
Teach thine armes then to embrace,
And sweet Rosie lips to kisse:
And mixe our soules in mutuall blisse.
Eyes were made for beauties grace,
Viewing, ruing Loves long paine:
Procur'd by beauties rude disdaine.

Come away, come sweet Love,
The golden morning wasts:
While the Sunne from his Sphere
His fierie arrowes casts,
Making all the shadowes flie,
Playing, staying in the Groave;
To entertaine the stealth of love.
Thither sweet Love let us hie
Flying, dying in desire:
Wing'd with sweet hopes and heavenly
    fire.

Come away, come sweet Love,
Doo not in vaine adjorne
Beauties grace that should rise
Like to the naked morne.
Lillies on the Rivers side,
And faire *Cyprian* flowers new blowne,
Desire no beauties but their owne.
Ornament is Nurse of pride,
Pleasure, measure, Loves delight:
Hast then sweet Love our wished flight.

Another of his Cinthia

AWAY with these selfe-loving-Lads,
Whom *Cupids* arrowe never glads.
Away poore soules that sigh and weepe,
In love of them that lie and sleepe,
  For *Cupid* is a Meadow God:
  And forceth none to kisse the rod.

God *Cupids* shaft like destenie,
Dooth eyther good or ill decree.
Desert is borne out of his bowe,
Reward upon his feete doth goe.
  What fooles are they that have not knowne,
  That Love likes no lawes but his owne?

My songs they be of *Cinthias* prayse,
I weare her Rings on Holly-dayes,
On every Tree I write her name,
And every day I reade the same.
  Where Honor, *Cupids* rivall is:
  There miracles are seene of his.

If *Cinthia* crave her ring of mee,
I blot her name out of the tree.
If doubt doe darken things held deere:
Then welfare nothing once a yeere.
> For many run, but one must win:
> Fooles onely hedge the Cuckoe in.

The worth that worthines should move,
Is love, which is the due of love.
And love as well the Sheepheard can,
As can the mightie Noble man.
> Sweet Nimph tis true, you worthy be,
> Yet without love, nought worth to me.

Another to his Cinthia

MY thoughts are winged with hopes, my hopes with
  love,
Mount love unto the Moone in cleerest night:
And say, as shee doth in the heavens move,
On earth so waines and wexeth my delight.
> And whisper this but softly in her eares:
> Hope oft doth hang the head, and trust shed
>   teares.

And you my thoughts that some mistrust doe carry,
If for mistrust my Mistrisse doe you blame:
Say, though you alter, yet you doe not varie,
As shee doth change, and yet remaine the same.
> Distrust doth enter harts, but not infect,
> And love is sweetest, seasoned with suspect.

If shee for this, with clowdes doe maske her eyes,
And make the heavens darke with her disdaine:
With windie sighes disperse them in the skyes,
Or with thy teares dissolve them into rayne.

Thoughts, hopes, and love, returne to me no more
Till *Cinthia* shine, as shee hath done before.

> *These three ditties were taken out of
> Maister* John Dowlands *books of table-
> ture for the Lute, the Authours names not
> there set downe, & therefore left to their
> owners*

Montanus *Sonnet in the woods*

ALAS, how wander I amidst these woods,
Whereas no day bright shine doth finde accesse?
But where the melancholy fleeting floods,
(Darke as the night) my night of woes expresse,
Disarmde of reason, spoyld of Natures goods,
Without redresse to salve my heavinesse
    I walke, whilst thought (too cruell to my harmes,)
    With endlesse greefe my heedlesse judgement
    charmes.

My silent tongue assailde by secrete feare,
My trayterous eyes imprisond in theyr joy:
My fatall peace devour'd in fained cheere,
My hart enforc'd to harbour in annoy.
My reason rob'd of power by yeelding care,
My fond opinions, slave to every joy.
    Oh Love, thou guide in my uncertaine way:
    Woe to thy bowe, thy fire, the cause of my decay.

S. E. D.

167

The Sheepheards sorrow, being disdained in love

MUSES helpe me, sorrow swarmeth,
Eyes are fraught with Seas of languish:
Haplesse hope my solace harmeth,
Mindes repast is bitter anguish.

Eye of day regarded never,
Certaine trust in world untrustie:
Flattering hope beguileth ever,
Wearie old, and wanton lustie.

Dawne of day beholds enthroned,
Fortunes darling proud and dreadlesse:
Darksome night dooth heare him moaned,
Who before was rich and needelesse.

Rob the Spheare of lines united,
Make a suddaine voide in nature:
Force the day to be benighted,
Reave the cause of time and creature.

Ere the world will cease to varie,
This I weepe for, this I sorrow:
Muses, if you please to tarie,
Further helpe I meane to borrow

Courted once by Fortunes favour,
Compast now with Envies curses:
All my thoughts of sorrowes savour,
Hopes runne fleeting like the Sourses.

Aye me, wanton scorne hath maimed
All the joyes my hart enjoyed:
Thoughts their thinking have disclaimed,
Hate my hopes have quite annoyed.

168

Scant regard my weale hath scanted,
Looking coy, hath forc'd my lowring:
Nothing lik'd, where nothing wanted,
Weds mine eyes to ceaselesse showring.

Former love was once admired,
Present favour is estraunged:
Loath'd the pleasure long desired,
Thus both men and thoughts are chaunged.

Lovely Swaine with luckie speeding,
Once, but now no more so friended:
You my Flocks have had in feeding,
From the morne, till day was ended.

Drink and fodder, foode and folding,
Had my Lambs and Ewes together:
I with them was still beholding,
Both in warmth and Winter weather.

Now they languish, since refused,
Ewes and Lambs are pain'd with pining:
I with Ewes and Lambs confused,
All unto our deaths declining.

Silence, leave thy Cave obscured,
Daigne a dolefull Swaine to tender:
Though disdaines I have endured,
Yet I am no deepe offender.

Phillips Sonne can with his finger
Hide his scarre, it is so little:
Little sinne a day to linger,
Wise men wander in a tittle.

Trifles yet my Swaine have turned,
Though my Sunne he never showeth:
Though I weepe, I am not mourned,
Though I want, no pittie groweth.

Yet for pittie, love my Muses,
Gentle silence be their cover:
They must leave their wonted uses,
Since I leave to be a Lover.

They shall live with thee enclosed,
I will loath my pen and paper:
Art shall never be supposed,
Sloth shall quench the watching Taper.

Kisse them silence, kisse them kindly,
Though I leave them, yet I love them:
Though my wit have led them blindly,
Yet a Swaine did once approve them.

I will travaile soiles removed,
Night and morning never merrie:
Thou shalt harbour that I loved,
I will love that makes me wearie.

If perchaunce the Sheepheard strayeth,
In thy walkes and shades unhaunted:
Tell the teene my hart betrayeth,
How neglect my joyes have daunted.

Thom. Lodge

A Pastorall Song betweene Phillis and Amarillis, two Nimphes, each aunswering other line for line

Fie on the sleights that men devise,
        heigh hoe sillie sleights:
When simple Maydes they would entice,
        Maides are young mens chiefe delights.
Nay, women they witch with their eyes,
        eyes like beames of burning Sunne:
And men once caught, they soone despise,
        so are Sheepheards oft undone.

If any young man win a maide,
        happy man is he:
By trusting him she is betraide,
        fie upon such treacherie.
If Maides win young men with their guiles,
        heigh hoe guilefull greefe:
They deale like weeping Crocodiles,
        that murther men without releefe.

I know a simple Country Hinde,
        heigh hoe sillie Swaine:
To whom faire *Daphne* prooved kinde,
        was he not kinde to her againe?
He vowed by *Pan* with many an oath,
        heigh hoe Sheepheards God is he:
Yet since hath chang'd, and broke his troath,
        troth-plight broke, will plagued be.

She had deceaved many a Swaine,
        fie on false deceite:
And plighted troath to them in vaine,
        there can be no greefe more great.

Her measure was with measure paide,
        heigh hoe, heigh hoe equall meede:
She was beguil'd that had betraide,
        so shall all deceavers speede.

If every Maide were like to me,
        heigh hoe hard of hart:
Both love and lovers scorn'd should be,
        scorners shall be sure of smart.
If every Maide were of my minde,
        heigh hoe, heigh hoe lovely sweete:
They to their Lovers should proove kinde,
        kindnes is for Maydens meete.

Me thinks love is an idle toy,
        heigh hoe busie paine:
Both wit and sence it dooth annoy,
        both sence & wit thereby we gaine.
Tush *Phillis* cease, be not so coy,
        heigh hoe, heigh hoe coy disdaine:
I know you love a Sheepheards boy,
        fie that Maydens so should faine.

Well *Amarillis*, now I yeeld,
        Sheepheards pipe aloude:
Love conquers both in towne and field,
        like a Tirant, fierce and proude.
The evening starre is up ye see,
        Vesper shines, we must away:
Would every Lover might agree,
        so we end our Roundelay.

                        H. C.

The Sheepheards Antheme

NEERE to a bancke with Roses set about,
Where prettie Turtles joyning bill to bill:
And gentle springs steale softly murmuring out,
Washing the foote of pleasures sacred hill.
  There little Love sore wounded lyes,
   his bow and arrowes broken:
  Bedewede with teares from *Venus* eyes,
   Oh that it should be spoken.

Beare him my hart, slaine with her scornfull eye,
Where sticks the arrow that poore hart did kill:
With whose sharpe pyle, yet will him ere he die,
About my hart to write his latest will.
  And bid him send it backe to mee,
   at instant of his dying:
  That cruell, cruell shee may see,
   my fayth and her denying.

His Hearse shall be a mournfull Cypres shade,
And for a Chauntrie, Philomels sweet lay:
Where prayer shall continually be made,
By Pilgrime lovers, passing by that way.
  With Nimphs and Sheepheards yeerely
   mone,
   his timelesse death beweeping:
  And telling that my hart alone,
   hath his last will in keeping.

        Mich. Drayton

pyle] *dart* or *arrow shaft*

The Countesse of Pembrookes Pastorall

A SHEEPHEARD and a Sheepheardesse,
    sate keeping sheepe upon the downes:
His lookes did gentle blood expresse,
    her beauty was no foode for clownes.
     Sweet lovely twaine, what might you be?

Two fronting hills bedect with flowers,
    they chose to be each others seate:
And there they stole theyr amorous houres,
    with sighes and teares, poore lovers meate,
     Fond Love that feed'st thy servants so.

Faire freend, quoth he, when shall I live,
    That am halfe dead, yet cannot die?
Can beautie such sharpe guerdon give,
    to him whose life hangs in your eye?
     Beautie is milde, and will not kill.

Sweet Swaine, quoth shee, accuse not mee,
    that long have been thy humble thrall:
But blame the angry destinie,
    whose kinde consent might finish all,
     Ungentle Fate, to crosse true love.

Quoth hee, let not our Parents hate,
    disjoyne what heaven hath linckt in one:
They may repent, and all too late
    if chyldlesse they be left alone.
     Father nor freend, should wrong true love.

The Parents frowne, said shee, is death,
    to children that are held in awe:
From them we drew our vitall breath,
    they challenge dutie then by law,
     Such dutie as kills not true love.

They have, quoth hee, a kinde of sway,
    on these our earthly bodies heere:
But with our soules deale not they may,
    the God of love doth hold them deere.
      Hee is most meet to rule true love.

I know, said shee, tis worse then hell,
    when Parents choyse must please our eyes:
Great hurt comes thereby, I can tell,
    forc'd love in desperate danger dies.
      Fayre mayde, then fancie thy true love.

If wee, quoth hee, might see the houre,
    of that sweet state which never ends,
Our heavenly gree might have the power,
    to make our Parents as deere freends.
      All rancour yeelds to soveraine love.

Then God of love, sayd shee, consent,
    and shew some wonder of thy power:
Our Parents, and our owne content,
    may be confirmde by such an houre.
      Graunt greatest God to further love.

The Fathers, who did always tend,
    when thus they got theyr private walke,
As happy fortune chaunc'd to send,
    unknowne to each, heard all this talke.
      Poore soules to be so crost in love.

Behind the hills whereon they sate,
    they lay this while and listned all:
And were so mooved both thereat,
    that hate in each began to fall.
      Such is the power of sacred love.

They shewed themselves in open sight,
>>poore Lovers, Lord how they were mazde?
And hand in hand the Fathers plight,
>>whereat (poore harts) they gladly gazde.
>>Hope now begins to further love.

And to confirme a mutuall band,
>>of love, that at no time should ceasse:
They likewise joyned hand in hand,
>>The Sheepheard and the Sheepheardesse.
>>Like fortune still befall true loue.

>>>>>>*Shep. Tonie*

gree] *goodwill*

Another of Astrophell

THE Nightingale so soone as Aprill bringeth
Unto her rested sence a perfect waking:
While late bare earth, proude of newe clothing
>>springeth,
Sings out her woes, a thorne her Song-booke making.
>>>And mournfully bewayling
>>>Her throate in tunes expresseth,
>>>What greefe her brest oppresseth,
>>>For *Tereus* force, on her chast will pre-
>>>>vailing.
>>Oh *Philamela* faire, oh take some gladnes,
>>That heere is juster cause of plaintfull sadnes.
>>Thine earth now springs, mine fadeth:
>>They thorne without, my thorne my hart in-
>>>vadeth.

Alas, shee hath no other cause of languish
But *Tereus* love, on her by strong hand wroken:

Wherein she suffering all her spirits languish,
Full woman-like complaines, her will was broken.
   But I, who daily craving,
   Cannot have to content mee:
   Have more cause to lament mee,
   Sith wanting is more woe, then too much
    having.
  Oh *Philamela* faire, oh take some gladnes,
  That heere is juster cause of plaintfull sadnes,
  Thine earth now springs, mine fadeth:
  They thorne without, my thorne my hart in-
    vadeth.

        S. Phil. Sidney

Faire Phillis *and her Sheepheard*

SHEEPHEARD, saw you not
   my faire lovely *Phillis*,
Walking on this mountaine,
   or on yonder plaine?
She is gone this way to *Dianaes* Fountaine,
   and hath left me wounded,
    with her high disdaine.
  Aye me, she is faire,
  And without compare,
   Sorrow come and sit with me:
  Love is full of feares,
  Love is full of teares,
    Love without these cannot be.
Thus my passions paine me,
For my love hath slaine me,
   Gentle Sheepheard beare a part:
Pray to *Cupids* mother,
For I know no other
   that can helpe to ease my smart.

Sheepheard, I have seene
  thy faire lovely *Phillis*
Where her flocks are feeding,
  by the Rivers side:
Oh, I must admire
  she so farre exceeding
In surpassing beautie,
  should surpasse in pride.
 But alas I finde,
 They are all unkinde
   Beauty knowes her power too well:
  When they list, they love,
  When they please, they move,
   thus they turne our heaven to hell.
For their faire eyes glauncing,
Like to *Cupids* dauncing,
  roule about still to deceave us:
With vaine hopes deluding,
Still dispraise concluding,
  Now they love, and now they leave us.

Thus I doo despaire,
  have her I shall never,
If she be so coy,
  lost is all my love:
But she is so faire
  I must love her ever,
All my paine is joy,
  which for her I prove.
 If I should her trie,
 And she should denie
   heavie hart with woe will breake:
 Though against my will
 Tongue thou must be still,
   for she will not heare thee speake.
Then with sighs goe proove her,
Let them shew I love her,
  gracious *Venus* be my guide:

But though I complaine me,
She will still disdaine me,
       beauty is so full of pride.

What though she be faire?
      speake, and feare not speeding,
Be she nere so coy,
      yet she may be wunne:
Unto her repaire,
      where her Flocks are feeding,
Sit and tick and toy
      till set be the Sunne.
   Sunne then being set,
   Feare not *Vulcanes* net,
     though that *Mars* therein was caught:
   If she doo denie
   Thus to her replie
     Venus lawes she must be taught.
Then with kisses moove her,
That's the way to proove her,
      thus thy *Phillis* must be wone:
She will not forsake thee,
But her Love will make thee,
      When Loves duty once is done.

Happie shall I be,
      If she graunt me favour,
Else for love I die
     Phillis is so faire:
Boldly then goe see,
      thou maist quickly have her,
Though she should denie,
      yet doo not despaire.
   She is full of pride,
   Venus be my guide,
     helpe a sillie Sheepheards speede:

179

Use no such delay,
Sheepheard, goe thy way,
     venture man and doo the deede.
I will sore complaine me,
Say that love hath slaine thee,
     if her favours doo not feede:
But take no deniall,
Stand upon thy triall,
     spare to speake, and want of speede.

tick] *dally*   *I. G.*

The Sheepheards Song of Venus *and* Adonis

VENUS faire did ride,
     silver Doves they drew her,
By the pleasant lawnds
     ere the Sunne did rise:
Vestaes beautie rich
     opend wide to view her,
Philomel records
     pleasing Harmonies.
     Every bird of spring
     cheerefully did sing,
          Paphos Goddesse they salute:
Now Loves Queene so faire,
     had of mirth no care,
         for her Sonne had made her mute.
In her breast so tender
He a shaft did enter,
     when her eyes beheld a boy:
Adonis was he named,
By his Mother shamed,
     yet he now is *Venus* joy.

180

Him alone she met,
        ready bound for hunting,
Him she kindly greetes,
        and his journey stayes:
Him she seekes to kisse
        no devises wanting,
Him her eyes still wooe,
        him her tongue still prayes.
    He with blushing red
    Hangeth downe the head,
        not a kisse can he afford:
    His face is turn'd away,
    Silence sayd her nay,
        still she woo'd him for a word.
    Speake shee said thou fairest,
    Beautie thou impairest,
      see mee, I am pale and wan:
    Lovers all adore mee,
    I for love implore thee,
        christall teares with that downe ran.

Him heere-with shee forc'd
        to come sit downe by her,
Shee his necke embrac'de
        gazing in his face:
Hee like one transformd
        stird no looke to eye her
Every hearbe did wooe him
        growing in that place.
        Each bird with a dittie,
            prayed him for pitty
                in behalfe of beauties Queene:
        Waters gentle murmour,
            craved him to love her,
                yet no liking could be seene.
    Boy shee sayd, looke on mee,
    Still I gaze upon thee,
            speake I pray thee my delight:
181

Coldly hee replyed,
And in breefe denyed,
      to bestow on her a sight.

I am now too young,
      to be wunne by beauty,
Tender are my yeeres
      I am yet a bud:
Fayre thou art, shee said
      then it is thy dutie,
Wert thou but a blossome
      to effect my good.
            Every beauteous flower,
                  boasteth in my power,
                        Byrds and beasts my lawes effect:
                  Mirrha thy faire mother,
                        most of any other,
                              did my lovely hests respect.
                  Be with me delighted,
                  Thou shalt be requited,
                        every Nimph on thee shall tend:
                  All the Gods shall love thee,
                  Man shall not reprove thee,
                        Love himselfe shall be thy freend.

Wend thee from me *Venus*,
      I am not disposed,
Thou wring'st mee too hard,
      pre-thee let me goe:
Fie, what a paine it is
      thus to be enclosed,
If love begin with labour,
      it will end in woe.
            kisse mee, I will leave,
                  heere a kisse receive,
                        a short kisse I doe it find:

182

Wilt thou leave me so?
　　yet thou shalt not goe,
　　　　breathe once more thy balmie wind.
It smelleth of the Mirh-tree,
That to the world did bring thee,
　　　　never was perfume so sweet:
When she had thus spoken,
Shee gave him a token,
　　　　and theyr naked bosoms meet.

Now hee sayd, let's goe,
　　harke, the hounds are crying,
Grieslie Boare is up,
　　Hunts-men follow fast:
At the name of Boare,
　　Venus seemed dying,
Deadly coloured pale,
　　Roses over-cast.
　　　　Speake sayd shee, no more,
　　　　　of following the Boare,
　　　　　　thou unfit for such a chase:
　　　　Course the fearefull Hare,
　　　　　Venson doe not spare,
　　　　　　if thou wilt yeeld *Venus* grace.
Shun the Boare I pray thee,
Else I still will stay thee,
　　　　herein he vowed to please her minde,
Then her armes enlarged,
Loth shee him discharged,
　　　　forth he went as swift as winde.

Thetis Phœbus Steedes
　　in the West retained,
Hunting sport was past,
　　Love her love did seeke:
Sight of him too soone
　　gentle Queene shee gained,

On the ground he lay
    blood had left his cheeke.
      For an orped Swine,
        smit him in the groyne,
          deadly wound his death did bring:
    Which when *Venus* found,
      shee fell in a swound,
        and awakte, her hands did wring.
Nimphs and Satires skipping,
Came together tripping,
      Eccho every cry exprest:
Venus by her power,
Turnd him to a flower,
      which shee weareth in her creast.

H. C.

orped] *fierce*

Thirsis *the Sheepheard his deaths song*

THIRSIS to die desired,
    marking her eyes that to his hart was neerest:
And shee that with his flame no lesse was fiered,
    sayd to him: Oh hart's love deerest:
      Alas, forbeare to die now,
      By thee I live, by thee I wish to die too.

Thirsis that heate refrained,
    wherewith to die poore lover then hee hasted,
Thinking it death while hee his lookes maintained,
    full fixed on her eyes, full of pleasure,
    and lovely Nectar sweet from them he tasted.
His daintie Nimph, that now at hand espyed
    the harvest of loves treasure,

Said thus, with eyes all trembling, faint and wasted:
    I die now,
The Sheepheard then replyed,
    and I sweet life doe die too.

Thus these two Lovers fortunately dyed,
    Of death so sweet, so happy, and so desired:
    That to die so againe their life retired.

> *Out of Maister* N. Young
> *his* Musica Transalpina

Another stanza added after

THIRSIS enjoyed the graces,
Of *Chloris* sweet embraces,
Yet both theyr joyes were scanted:
    For darke it was, and candle-light they wanted,
Wherewith kinde *Cinthia* in the heaven that shined,
    her nightly vaile resigned,
    and her faire face disclosed.
    Then each from others lookes such joy derived:
    That both with meere delight dyed, and revived.

Another Sonet thence taken

ZEPHIRUS brings the time that sweetly senteth
    with flowers and hearbs, which Winters frost
      exileth:
Progne now chirpeth, *Philomel* lamenteth,
    Flora the Garlands white and red compileth:

Fields doo rejoyce, the frowning skie relenteth,
　　Jove to behold his dearest daughter smileth:
The ayre, the water, the earth to joy consenteth,
　　each creature now to love him reconcileth.
But with me wretch, the stormes of woe persever,
　　and heavie sighs which from my hart she straineth
That tooke the key thereof to heaven for ever,
　　so that singing of birds, and spring-times flowring:
And Ladies love that mens affection gaineth,
　　are like a Desert, and cruell beasts devouring.

The Sheepheards slumber

In Pescod time, when Hound to horne,
　　gives eare till Buck be kild:
And little Lads with pipes of corne,
　　sate keeping beasts a field.
I went to gather Strawberies tho,
　　by Woods and Groaves full faire:
And parcht my face with *Phœbus* so,
　　in walking in the ayre.
That downe I layde me by a streame,
　　with boughs all over-clad:
And there I met the straungest dreame,
　　That ever Sheepheard had.
Me thought I saw each Christmas game,
　　each revell all and some:
And every thing that I can name,
　　or may in fancie come.
The substance of the sights I saw,
　　in silence passe they shall:
Because I lack the skill to draw,
　　the order of them all.
But *Venus* shall not passe my pen,
　　whose maydens in disdaine:

Did feed upon the harts of men,
    that *Cupids* bowe had slaine.
And that blinde boy was all in blood,
    be-bath'd to the eares:
And like a Conquerour he stood,
    and scorned Lovers teares.
I have (quoth he) more harts at call,
    then *Cæsar* could commaund:
And like the Deare I make them fall,
    that runneth o're the lawnd.
One drops downe heere, another there,
    in bushes as they groane;
I bend a scornfull carelesse eare,
    to heare them make their moane.
Ah Sir (quoth *Honest Meaning*) then,
    thy boy-like brags I heare:
When thou hast wounded many a man,
    as Hunts-man doth the Deare.
Becomes it thee to triumph so?
    thy Mother wills it not:
For she had rather breake thy bowe,
    then thou shouldst play the sot.
What saucie merchant speaketh now,
    sayd *Venus* in her rage:
Art thou so blinde thou knowest not how
    I governe every age?
My Sonne doth shoote no shaft in wast,
    to me the boy is bound:
He never found a hart so chast,
    but he had power to wound,
Not so faire Goddesse (quoth *Free-will,*)
    in me there is a choise:
And cause I am of mine owne ill,
    if I in thee rejoyce.
And when I yeeld my selfe a slave,
    to thee, or to thy Sonne:
Such recompence I ought not have,
    if things be rightly done.

Why foole stept forth *Delight*, and said,
    when thou art conquer'd thus:
Then loe dame *Lust*, that wanton maide,
    thy Mistresse is iwus.
And *Lust* is *Cupids* darling deere,
    behold her where she goes:
She creepes the milk-warme flesh so neere,
    she hides her under close.
Where many privie thoughts doo dwell,
    a heaven heere on earth:
For they have never minde of hell,
    they thinke so much on mirth.
Be still *Good Meaning*, quoth *Good Sport*,
    let *Cupid* triumph make:
For sure his Kingdome shall be short
    if we no pleasure take.
Faire *Beautie*, and her play-feares gay,
    the virgins *Vestalles* too:
Shall sit and with their fingers play,
    as idle people doo,
If *Honest Meaning* fall to frowne,
    and I *Good Sport* decay:
Then *Venus* glory will come downe,
    and they will pine away.
Indeede (quoth *Wit*) this your device,
    with straungenes must be wrought,
And where you see these women nice,
    and looking to be sought:
With scowling browes their follies check,
    and so give them the Fig:
Let *Fancie* be no more at beck,
    when *Beautie* lookes so big.
When *Venus* heard how they conspir'd,
    to murther women so:
Me thought indeede the house was fier'd,
    with stormes and lightning tho.
The thunder-bolt through windowes burst.
    and in their steps a wight:

Which seem'd some soule or sprite accurst,
  so ugly was the sight.
I charge you Ladies all (quoth he)
  looke to your selves in hast:
For if that men so wilfull be,
  and have their thoughts so chast;
And they can tread on *Cupids* brest,
  and martch on *Venus* face:
Then they shall sleepe in quiet rest,
  when you shall waile your case.
With that had *Venus* all in spight,
  stir'd up the Dames to ire:
And *Lust* fell cold, and *Beautie* white,
  sate babling with *Desire*.
Whose mutt'ring words I might not marke,
  much whispering there arose:
The day did lower, the Sunne wext darke,
  away each Lady goes.
But whether went this angry flock,
  our Lord him-selfe doth know:
Where-with full lowdly crewe the Cock,
  and I awaked so.
A dreame (quoth I?) a dogge it is,
  I take thereon no keepe:
I gage my head, such toyes as this,
  dooth spring from lack of sleepe.

          Ignoto

tho] *then* iwus] *certainly* Fig] *a contemptuous gesture*
tho] *then* keepe] *heed*

In wonted walkes, since wonted fancies change,
Some cause there is, which of strange cause doth rise:
For in each thing whereto my minde doth range,
Part of my paine me seems engraved lies.

The Rockes which were of constant minde, the marke
In climbing steepe, now hard refusall show:
The shading woods seeme now my sunne to darke,
And stately hils disdaine to looke so low.

The restfull Caves, now restlesse visions give,
In dales I see each way a hard assent:
Like late mowne Meades, late cut from joy I live,
Alas, sweet Brookes, doe in my teares augment.
    Rocks, woods, hills, caves, dales, meades brookes
      aunswere mee:
    Infected mindes infect each thing they see.

                  S. Phil. Sidney

Of disdainfull Daphne

SHALL I say that I love you,
    Daphne disdainfull?
Sore it costs as I prove you,
    loving is painfull.

Shall I say what doth greeve mee?
    Lovers lament it:
Daphne will not releeve mee,
    late I repent it.

Shall I dye, shall I perrish,
    through her unkindnes?
Love untaught love to cherrish,
    sheweth his blindnes.

Shall the hills, shall the valleye,
    the fieldes the Cittie,
With the sound of my out-cryes,
    move her to pittie?

The deepe falls of fayre Rivers,
    and the windes turning:
Are the true musique givers,
    unto my mourning.

Where my flocks daily feeding,
    pining for sorrow:
At their maisters hart bleeding,
    shot with Loves arrow.

From her eyes to my hart-string,
    was the shaft launced:
It made all the woods to ring,
    by which it glaunced.

When this Nimph had usde me so,
    then she did hide her:
Haplesse I did *Daphne* know,
    haplesse I spyed her.

Thus Turtle-like I waild me,
    for my loves loosing:
Daphnes trust thus did faile me,
    woe worth such chusing.

M. H. Nowell

The passionate Sheepheard to his love

COME live with mee, and be my love,
And we will all the pleasures prove,
That Vallies, groves, hills and fieldes,
Woods, or steepie mountaine yeeldes.

And wee will sit upon the Rocks,
Seeing the Sheepheards feede theyr flocks,
By shallow Rivers, to whose falls,
Melodious byrds sing Madrigalls.

And I will make thee beds of Roses,
And a thousand fragrant poesies,
A cap of flowers, and a kirtle,
Imbroydred all with leaves of Mirtle.

A gowne made of the finest wooll,
Which from our pretty Lambes we pull,
Fayre lined slippers for the cold:
With buckles of the purest gold.

A belt of straw, and Ivie buds,
With Corall clasps and Amber studs,
And if these pleasures may thee move,
Come live with mee, and be my love.

The Sheepheards Swaines shall daunce & sing,
For thy delight each May-morning,
If these delights thy minde may move;
Then live with mee, and be my love.

Chr. Marlow

The Nimphs reply to the Sheepheard

If all the world and love were young,
And truth in every Sheepheards tongue,
These pretty pleasures might me move,
To live with thee, and be thy love.

Time drives the flocks from field to fold,
When Rivers rage, and Rocks grow cold,
And *Philomell* becommeth dombe,
The rest complaines of cares to come.

The flowers doe fade, & wanton fieldes,
To wayward winter reckoning yeeldes,
A honny tongue, a hart of gall,
Is fancies spring, but sorrowes fall.

Thy gownes, thy shooes, thy beds of Roses,
Thy cap, thy kirtle, and thy poesies,
Soone breake, soone wither, soone forgotten:
In follie ripe, in reason rotten.

Thy belt of straw and Ivie buddes,
Thy Corall claspes and Amber studdes,
All these in mee no meanes can move,
To come to thee, and be thy love.

But could youth last, and love still breede,
Had joyes no date, nor age no neede,
Then these delights my minde might move,
To live with thee, and be thy love.

Ignoto

193

Another of the same nature, made since

Come live with mee, and be my deere,
And we will revell all the yeere,
In plaines and groaves, on hills and dales:
Where fragrant ayre breedes sweetest gales.

There shall you have the beauteous Pine,
The Cedar, and the spreading Vine,
And all the woods to be a Skreene:
Least *Phœbus* kisse my Sommers Queene.

The seate for your disport shall be
Over some River in a tree,
Where silver sands, and pebbles sing,
Eternall ditties with the spring.

There shall you see the Nimphs at play,
And how the Satires spend the day,
The fishes gliding on the sands:
Offering their bellies to your hands.

The birds with heavenly tuned throates,
Possesse woods Ecchoes with sweet noates,
Which to your sences will impart,
A musique to enflame the hart.

Upon the bare and leafe-lesse Oake,
The Ring-Doves wooings will provoke
A colder blood then you possesse,
To play with me and doo no lesse.

In bowers of Laurell trimly dight,
We will out-weare the silent night,
While *Flora* busie is to spread:
Her richest treasure on our bed.

Ten thousand Glow-wormes shall attend,
And all their sparkling lights shall spend,
All to adorne and beautifie:
Your lodging with most majestie.

Then in mine armes will I enclose
Lillies faire mixture with the Rose,
Whose nice perfections in loves play:
Shall tune me to the highest key.

Thus as we passe the welcome night,
In sportfull pleasures and delight,
The nimble Fairies on the grounds,
Shall daunce and sing mellodious sounds.

If these may serve for to entice,
Your presence to Loves Paradice,
Then come with me, and be my Deare:
And we will straite begin the yeare.

Ignoto

The Wood-mans walke

THROUGH a faire Forrest as I went
              upon a Sommers day,
I met a Wood-man queint and gent,
              yet in a strange aray.
I mervail'd much at his disguise,
              whom I did know so well:
But thus in tearmes both grave and wise,
              his minde he gan to tell.
Friend, muse not at this fond aray,
              but list a while to me:

195

For it hath holpe me to survay
        what I shall shew to thee.
Long liv'd I in this Forrest faire,
        till wearie of my weale:
Abroade in walks I would repaire,
        as now I will reveale.
My first dayes walke was to the Court,
        where Beautie fed mine eyes:
Yet found I that the Courtly sport,
        did maske in slie disguise.
For falshood sate in fairest lookes,
        and friend to friend was coy:
Court-favour fill'd but empty bookes,
        and there I found no joy.
Desert went naked in the cold,
        when crouching craft was fed:
Sweet words were cheaply bought and sold,
        but none that stood in sted,
Wit was imployed for each mans owne,
        plaine meaning came too short:
All these devises seene and knowne,
        made me forsake the Court.
Unto the Citty next I went,
        in hope of better hap:
Where liberally I launch'd and spent,
        as set on Fortunes lap.
The little stock I had in store,
        me thought would nere be done:
Friends flockt about me more and more,
        as quickly lost as wone.
For when I spent, they then were kinde,
        but when my purse did faile:
The formost man came last behinde,
        thus love with wealth doth quaile.
Once more for footing yet I strove,
        although the world did frowne:
But they before that held me up,
        together troad me downe.

And least once more I should arise,
   they sought my quite decay:
Then got I into this disguise,
   and thence I stole away.
And in my minde (me thought) I saide,
   Lord blesse me from the Cittie:
Where simplenes is thus betraide,
   and no remorce or pittie.
Yet would I not give over so,
   but once more trie my fate:
And to the Country then I goe,
   to live in quiet state.
There did appeare no subtile showes,
   but yea and nay went smoothly:
But Lord how Country-folks can glose,
   when they speake most soothly.
More craft was in a buttond cap,
   and in an old wives rayle:
Then in my life it was my hap,
   to see on Downe or Dale.
There was no open forgerie,
   but under-handed gleaning:
Which they call Country pollicie,
   but hath a worser meaning.
Some good bold-face beares out the wrong,
   because he gaines thereby:
The poore mans back is crackt ere long,
   yet there he lets him lye.
And no degree among them all,
   but had such close intending:
That I upon my knees did fall,
   and prayed for their amending.
Back to the woods I got againe,
   in minde perplexed sore:
Where I found ease of all this paine,
   and meane to stray no more.
There, Citty, Court, nor Country too,
   can any way annoy me:

But as a wood-man ought to doo,
        I freely may imploy me.
There live I quietly alone,
        and none to trip my talke:
Wherefore when I am dead and gone,
        think on the Wood-mans walke.

Shep. Tonie

queint old form of quaint] wise or skilled
gent] courteous   rayle] neck-cloth

Thirsis *the Sheepheard, to his Pipe*

LIKE Desert woods, with darksome shades obscured,
Where dreadfull beasts, where hatefull horror raigneth
Such is my wounded hart, whom sorrow payneth,

The Trees are fatall shaft, to death inured,
That cruell love within my breast maintaineth,
To whet my greefe, when as my sorrow wayneth.

The ghastly beasts, my thoughts in cares assured,
Which wage me warre, while hart no succour gaineth:
With false suspect, and feare that still remaineth.

The horrors, burning sighs by cares procured,
Which foorth I send, whilst weeping eye complaineth:
To coole the heate, the helplesse hart containeth.

But shafts, but cares, but sighs, horrors unrecured,
Were nought esteem'd, if for these paines awarded:
My faithfull love by her might be regarded.

Ignoto

198

An excellent Sonnet of a Nimph

VERTUE, beauty, and speach, did strike, wound,
      charme,
My hart, eyes, eares, with wonder, love, delight:
First, second, last, did binde, enforce, and arme,
His works, showes, sutes, with wit, grace, and vowes-
      might.

Thus honour, liking, trust, much, farre, and deepe,
Held, pearst, possest, my judgement, scence, and will;
Till wrongs, contempt, deceite, did grow, steale,
      creepe
Bands, favour, faith, to breake, defile, and kill.

Then greefe, unkindnes, proofe, tooke, kindled, taught,
Well grounded, noble, due, spite, rage, disdaine:
But ah, alas, (in vaine) my minde, sight, thought,
Dooth him, his face, his words, leave, shunne, refraine.
  For nothing, time, nor place, can loose, quench,
      ease:
  Mine owne, embraced, sought, knot, fire, disease.

S. Phil. Sidney

A Report Song in a dreame, betweene a Sheepheard and his Nimph

SHALL we goe daunce the hay?   The hay?
Never pipe could ever play
    better Sheepheards Roundelay.

Shall we goe sing the Song?   The Song?
Never Love did ever wrong:
    faire Maides hold hands all a-long

Shall we goe learne to woo?   To woo?
Never thought came ever too,
    better deede could better doo.

Shall we goe learne to kisse?   To kisse?
Never hart could ever misse
    comfort, where true meaning is.

Thus at base they run,   They run,
When the sport was scarse begun:
    but I wakt, and all was done.

N. Breton.

Another of the same

SAY that I should say, I love ye?
    would you say, tis but a saying?
But if Love in prayers moove ye?
    will not you be moov'd with praying?

Think I think that Love should know ye?
    will you thinke, tis but a thinking?
But if Love the thought doo show ye,
    will ye loose your eyes with winking?

Write that I doo write you blessed,
    will you write, tis but a writing?
But if truth and Love confesse it:
    will ye doubt the true enditing?

No, I say, and thinke, and write it,
    write, and thinke, and say your pleasure:
Love, and truth, and I endite it,
    you are blessed out of measure.

N. Breton

The Sheepheards conceite of Prometheus

PROMETHEUS, when first from heaven hie,
He brought downe fire, ere then on earth unseene:
Fond of delight, a Satyre standing by,
Gave it a kisse, as it like sweete had beene.

Feeling forth-with the other burning power,
Wood with the smart, with shoutes and shrikings
      shrill:
He sought his ease in River, field, and bower,
But for the time his greefe went with him still.

So silly I, with that unwonted sight,
In humane shape, an Angell from above:
Feeding mine eyes, th'impression there did light,
That since I runne, and rest as pleaseth Love.
      The difference is, the Satires lips, my hart:
      He for a while, I evermore have smart.

                    S. E. D.

Another of the same

A SATYRE once did runne away for dread,
   with sound of horne, which he him-selfe did blow:
Fearing, and feared thus, from him-selfe he fled,
   deeming strange evill in that he did not know.

Such causelesse feares, when coward minds doo take,
   it makes them flie that, which they faine would have:
As this poore beast, who did his rest forsake,
   thinking not why, but how him-selfe to save.

Even thus mought I, for doubts which I conceave
    of mine owne words, mine owne good hap betray:
And thus might I, for feare of may be, leave
    the sweet pursute of my desired pray.
        Better like I thy Satire, dearest *Dyer*:
        Who burnt his lips, to kisse faire shining fier.

S. Phil. Sidney

mought] *might*

The Sheepheards Sunne

FAIRE Nimphs, sit ye heere by me,
    on this flowrie greene:
While we this merrie day doo see,
    some things but sildome seene.
Sheepheards all, now come sit a-round,
    on yond checquered plaine:
While from the woods we heere resound,
        some comfort for Loves paine.
        Every bird sits on his bowe,
        As brag as he that is the best:
        Then sweet Love, reveale howe
            our minds may be at rest?
        Eccho thus replyed to mee,
        Sit under yonder Beechen tree,
        And there Love shall shew thee
            how all may be redrest.

Harke, harke, harke the Nightingale,
    in her mourning lay:
Shee tells her stories wofull tale,
    to warne yee if shee may.

Faire maydes, take yee heede of love,
    it is a perlous thing:
As *Philomele* her selfe did prove,
    abused by a King.
        If Kings play false, beleeve no men,
        That make a seemely outward show:
        But caught once, beware then,
          for then begins your woe.
        They will looke babies in your eyes,
        And speake so faire as faire may be,
        But trust them in no wise,
          example take by mee.

Fie, fie, said the Threstle-cocke,
    you are much too blame:
For one mans fault, all men to blot,
    impayring theyr good name.
Admit you were usde amisse,
    by that ungentle King,
It followes not that you for this,
    should all mens honours wring.
        There be good, and there be bad,
        And some are false, and some are true:
        As good choyse is still had
          amongst us men, as you.
        Women have faultes as well as wee,
        Some say for our one, they have three.
        Then smite not, nor bite not,
          when you as faultie be.

Peace, peace, quoth Madge-Howlet then,
    sitting out of sight:
For women are as good as men,
    and both are good alike.
Not so, said the little Wrenne,
    difference there may be:
The Cocke alway commaunds the Hen:
    then men shall goe for mee.

Then Robin-Redbrest stepping in,
Would needs take up this tedious strife,
Protesting, true-loving,
   In either lengthened life.
If I love you, and you love mee,
Can there be better harmonie?
Thus ending, contending,
   Love must the umpiere be.

Faire Nimphs, Love must be your guide,
   chast, unspotted love:
To such as doe your thralles betyde,
   resolv'de without remove.
Likewise jolly Sheepheard Swaines
   if you doe respect,
The happy issue of your paines,
   true love must you direct.
      You heare the birds contend for love,
      The bubling springs do sing sweet love,
      The Mountaines and Fountaines
        do Eccho nought but love.
Take hands then Nimphes & Sheepheards all,
And to this Rivers musiques fall
Sing true love, and chast love
   begins our Festivall.

Shep. Tonie

brag] *lively*

Colin *the enamoured Sheepheard, singeth this passion of love*

O GENTLE Love, ungentle for thy deede,
   thou makest my hart,
   a bloodie marke,
   With piercing shot to bleede.

204

Shoote soft sweete Love, for feare thou shoote amisse,
       for feare too keene,
        thy arrowes beene:
   And hit the hart, where my beloved is.

Too faire that fortune were, nor never I
       shall be so blest,
        among the rest:
   That love shal ceaze on her by simpathy.

Then since with Love my prayers beare no boote,
       this doth remaine,
        to ease my paine,
   I take the wound, and die at *Venus* foote.

                      Geo. Peele

Oenones *complaint in blanke verse*

MELPOMENE the Muse of tragicke songs,
With mournfull tunes in stole of dismall hue,
Assist a sillie Nimphe to waile her woe,
   And leave thy lustie company behind.

Thou lucklesse wreathe becomes not me to weare,
The Poplar tree for tryumph of my love,
Then as my joy, my pride of love is left;
   Be thou uncloathed of thy lovely greene.

And in thy leaves my fortunes written be,
And then some gentle winde let blow abroade,
That all the world may see, how false of love,
   False *Paris* hath to his *Oenone* beene.

                      Geo. Peele

stole] *a long robe*

The Sheepheards Consort

HARKE jollie Sheepheards,
    harke yond lustie ringing:
How cheerefully the bells daunce,
    the whilst the Lads are springing?
    Goe we then, why sit we here delaying:
    And all yond mery wanton lasses playing?
      How gailie *Flora* leades it,
        and sweetly treads it?
      The woods and groaves they ring,
        lovely resounding:
      With Ecchoes sweet rebounding.

Out of Ma. Morleys Madrigals

Englands

H E L I C O N

1614

———

An Invective against Love

ALL is not golde that shineth bright in show,
Not every flowre so good, as faire, to sight,
The deepest streames, above doe calmest flow,
And strongest poisons oft the taste delight,
    The pleasant baite doth hide the harmfull hooke,
    And false deceit can lend a friendly looke.

Love is the gold whose outward hew doth passe,
Whose first beginnings goodly promise make
Of pleasures faire, and fresh as Sommers grasse,
Which neither Sunne can parch, nor winde can shake:
    But when the mould should in the fire be tride,
    The gold is gone, the drosse doth still abide.

Beautie the flowre, so fresh, so faire, so gay,
So sweet to smell, so soft to touch and tast:
As seemes it should endure, by right, for aye,
And never be with any storme defast,
    But when the baleful Southerne wind doth blow,
    Gone is the glory which it erst did shew.

Love is the streame, whose waves so calmely flow
As might intice mens minds to wade therein:
Love is the poison mixt with sugar so,
As might by outward sweetnesse liking win,
    But as the deepe ore'flowing stops thy breath,
    So poyson once receiv'd brings certaine death.

Love is the baite, whose taste the fish deceives,
And makes them swallow downe the choking hooke,
Love is the face whose fairnesse judgement reaves,
And makes thee trust a false and fained looke.
    But as the hooke the foolish fish dooth kill,
    So flatt'ring lookes, the lovers life doth spill.

Dispraise of Love, and Lovers follies

If Love be life, I long to die,
    Live they that list for me:
And he that gaines the most thereby,
    A foole at least shall be.
But he that feeles the sorest fits,
Scapes with no lesse than losse of wits,
    Unhappy life they gaine,
    Which Love doe entertaine.

In day by fained lookes they live,
    By lying dreames in night,
Each frowne a deadly wound doth give,
    Each smile a false delight.
If't hap their Lady pleasant seeme,
It is for others love they deeme:
    If voide she seeme of joy,
    Disdaine doth make her coy.

Such is the peace that Lovers finde,
    Such is the life they leade.
Blowne here and there with every winde
    Like flowers in the Mead.
Now warre, now peace, now warre againe,
Desire, despaire, delight, disdaine,
    Though dead in midst of life,
    In peace, and yet at strife.

                        Ignoto

Two Pastorals, upon three friends meeting

JOYNE mates in mirth to me,
Grant pleasure to our meeting:
Let Pan our good God see,
How gratefull is our greeting.
    Joyne hearts and hands, so let it be.
    Make but one minde in bodies three.

Ye Hymnes and singing skill
Of God *Apolloes* giving,
Be prest our reeds to fill,
With sound of musicke living.
    Joyne hearts and hands, &c.

Sweet *Orpheus* Harpe, whose sound
The stedfast mountaines moved,
Let here thy skill abound,
To joyne sweet friends beloved.
    Joyne hearts and hands, &c.

My two and I be met,
A happy blessed Trinitie,
As three most joyntly set,
In firmest band of unitie.
    Joyne hearts and hands, &c.

Welcome my two to me,
The number best beloved,
Within my heart you be
In friendship unremoved.
 Joyne hands, &c.

Give leave your flocks to range,
Let us the while be playing,
Within the Elmy grange,
Your flocks will not be straying.
 Joyne hands, &c.

Cause all the mirth you can,
Since I am now come hither,
Who never joy but when
I am with you together.
 Joyne hands, &c.

Like lovers doe their love,
So joy I in your seeing:
Let nothing me remove
From alwaies with you being.
 Joyne hands, &c.

And as the turtle Dove
To mate with whom he liveth,
Such comfort, fervent love
Of you to my heart giveth.
 Joyne hands, &c.

Now joyned be our hands,
Let them be ne're asunder,
But linkt in binding bands
By metamorphoz'd wonder.
 *So should our severed bodies three
As one for ever joyned be.*

    S. Phil. Sidney

An Heroicall Poeme

My wanton Muse that whilome wont to sing,
Faire beauties praise and Venus sweet delight,
Of late hath chang'd the tenor of her string
To higher tunes than serve for Cupids fight.
    Shrill Trumpets sound, sharpe swords, and
      Lances strong,
    Warre, bloud and death, were matter of her
      song.

The God of Love by chance had heard thereof,
That I was prov'd a rebell to his crowne,
Fit words for warre, quoth he, with angry scoffe,
A likely man to write of Mars his frowne.
    Well are they sped whose praises he shall write,
    Whose wanton Pen can nought but love indite.

This said, he whiskt his party-colour'd wings,
And downe to earth he comes more swift then
      thought,
Then to my heart in angry haste he flings,
To see what change these newes of warres had
      wrought.
    He pries, and lookes, he ransacks every vaine,
    Yet finds he nought, save love, and lovers paine.

Then I that now perceiv'd his needlesse feare,
With heavie smile began to plead my cause:
In vaine (quoth I) this endlesse griefe I beare,
In vaine I strive to keepe thy grievous Lawes,
    If after proofe, so often trusty found,
    Unjust suspect condemne me as unsound.

Is this the guerdon of my faithfull heart?
Is this the hope on which my life is staide?
Is this the ease of never-ceasing smart?
Is this the price that for my paines is paide?
> Yet better serve fierce Mars in bloudie field,
> Where death, or conquest, end or joy doth
> yeeld.

Long have I serv'd, what is my pay but paine?
Oft have I sude, what gaine I but delay?
My faithfull love is quited with disdaine,
My griefe a game, my pen is made a play.
> Yea love that doth in other favour finde,
> In me is counted madnesse out of kinde.

And last of all, but grievous most of all,
Thy self, sweet love, hath kild me with suspect:
Could love beleeve, that I from love would fall?
Is warre of force to make me love neglect.
> No, Cupid knowes, my minde is faster set,
> Than that by warre I should my love forget.

My Muse indeed to warre enclines her minde,
The famous acts of worthy *Brute* to write:
To whom the Gods this Ilands rule assignde,
Which long he sought by Seas through Neptunes
> spight,
> With such conceits my busie head doth swell.
> But in my heart nought else but love doth dwell.

And in this warre thy part is not the least,
Here shall my Muse *Brutes* noble Love declare:
Here shalt thou see thy double love increast,
Of fairest twins that ever Lady bare:
> Let Mars triumph in armour shining bright,
> His conquerd armes shall be thy triumphs light.

As he the world, so thou shalt him subdue,
And I thy glory through the world will ring,
So by my paines, thou wilt vouchsafe to rue,
And kill despaire. With that he whiskt his wing.
    And bid me write, and promist wished rest,
    But sore I feare false hope will be the best.

Ignoto

The Lovers absence kils me, her presence kils me

THE frozen snake, opprest with heaped snow
By strugling hard gets out her tender head,
And spies farre off from where she lies below
The winter Sunne that from the North is fled.
    But all in vaine she lookes upon the light,
    Where heate is wanting to restore her might.

What doth it helpe a wretch in prison pent,
Long time with biting hunger over-prest,
To see without, or smell within, the sent,
Of daintie fare for others tables drest?
    Yet Snake and pris'ner both behold the thing,
    The which (but not with sight) might comfort
      bring.

Such is my state, or worse if worse may be,
My hart opprest with heavie frost of care,
Debar'd of that which is most deere to me,
Kild up with cold, and pinde with evill fare,
    And yet I see the thing might yeelde reliefe,
    And yet the sight doth breed my greater griefe.

So *Thisbe* saw her Lover through the wall,
And saw thereby she wanted that she saw,
And so I see, and seeing want withall,
And wanting so, unto my death I draw.
    And so my death were twenty times my friend,
    If with this verse my hated life might end.

                            Ignoto

'kils' in the second line of the title of the above poem
was emended to 'cures' by Bullen

Love the only price of love

THE fairest Pearles that Northerne Seas doe breed,
For precious stones from Easterne coasts are sold.
Nought yields the earth that from exchange is freed,
Gold values all, and all things value Gold.
    Where goodnes wants an equall change to make,
    There greatnesse serves, or number place doth
        take.

No mortall thing can beare so high a price,
But that with mortall thing it may be bought,
The corne of Sicill buies the Westerne spice,
French wine of us, of them our cloath is sought.
    No pearles, no gold, no stones, no corne, no
        spice.
    No cloath, no wine, of love can pay the price.

What thing is love, which nought can countervaile?
Nought save itself, ev'n such a thing is love.
All worldly wealth in worth as farre doth faile,
As lowest earth doth yeeld to heav'n above.
    Divine is love, and scorneth worldly pelfe,
    And can be bought with nothing, but with selfe.

Such is the price my loving heart would pay,
Such is the pay thy love doth claime as due.
Thy due is love, which I (poore I) assay,
In vaine assay to quite with friendship true:
     True is my love, and true shall ever be,
     And truest love is farre too base for thee.

Love but thy selfe, and love thy self alone,
For save thy self, none can thy love requite:
All mine thou hast, but all as good as none,
My small desart must take a lower flight.
     Yet if thou wilt vouchsafe my heart such blisse,
     Accept it for thy prisoner as it is.

                     Ignoto

Thyrsis *praise of his Mistresse*

ON a hill that grac'd the plaine
Thyrsis sate, a comely *Swaine*,
    Comelier Swaine nere grac'd a hill:
Whilst his Flocke that wandred nie
Cropt the greene grasse busilie,
    Thus he tun'd his Oaten quill.

Ver hath made the pleasant field
Many sev'rall odours yield,
    Odors aromaticall;
From fair *Astra's* cherrie lip,
Sweeter smells for ever skip,
    They in pleasing passen all.

Leavie Groves now mainely ring,
With each sweet birds sonnetting,
    Notes that make the *Eccho's* long:

But when *Astra* tunes her voyce,
All the mirthfull birds rejoyce,
    And are list'ning to her Song.

Fairely spreads the *Damaske Rose*,
Whose rare mixture doth disclose
    Beauties, pensils cannot faine:
Yet if *Astra* passe the bush,
Roses have been seene to blush,
    She doth all their beauties staine.

Phoebus shining bright in skie
Gilds the floods, heates mountaines hie,
    With his beames all-quickning fire:
Astra's eyes, (most sparkling ones)
Strikes a heate in hearts of stones,
    And enflames them with desire.

Fields are blest with flowrie wreath,
Ayre is blest when she doth breath,
    Birds make happy ev'ry Grove,
She each Bird when she doth sing;
Phoebus heate to earth doth bring,
    Shee makes Marble fall in love.
Those, *blessings* of the earth, we *Swaines* doe call;
Astra can *blesse* those *blessings earth* and all.

                       W. Browne

A defiance to disdainefull Love

Now have I learn'd with much adoe at last,
    By true disdaine to kill desire,
This was the marke at which I shot so fast,
    Unto this height I did aspire.
Proud Love, now doe thy worst, and spare not,
For thee and all thy shafts I care not.

What hast thou left wherewith to move my minde?
    What life to quicken dead desire?
I count thy wordes and oathes as light as winde,
    I feele no heate in all thy fire.
Goe change thy bow, and get a stronger,
Goe breake thy shafts, and buy thee longer.

In vaine thou bait'st thy hooke with beauties blaze,
    In vaine thy wanton eyes allure.
These are but toyes, for them that love to gaze,
    I know what harme thy lookes procure:
Some strange conceit must be devised,
Or thou and all thy skill despised.

Ignoto

An Epithalamium; or a Nuptiall Song, Applied to the Ceremonies of Marriage

Sunne rising

AURORA'S Blush (the Ensigne of the Day)
Hath wak't the God of Light, from *Tythons* bowre,
Who on our Bride, and Bride-groome doth display
His golden Beames, auspitious to this Howre.

219

Strewing of Flowers

Now busie Maydens strew sweet Flowres,
Much like our Bride in Virgin state;
    Now fresh, then prest, soone dying,
The death is sweet, and must be yours,
Time goes on Croutches till that date,
    Birds fledg'd must needes be flying.
Leade on whiles *Phoebus* Lights, and *Hymens* Fires,
Enflame each Heart with Zeale to Loves Desires.
    Chorus. Io to *Hymen Pæans* sing
        To *Hymen*, and my *Muses* King.

Going to Church. Bride Boyes

Forth honour'd Groome; behold, not farre behind
Your willing Bride; led by two strengthlesse Boyes;
For Venus Doves, or Thred but single twin'd,
May draw a Virgin, light in Marriage Joyes:
    Vesta growes pale, her Flame expires
    As yee come under *Junos* Phane,
        To offer at *Joves* Shrine
    The simpathie of *Hearts* desires
    Knitting the Knot, that doth containe
        Two soules, in Gordian Twine.
The Rites are done; and now, (as 'tis the guise)
Loves Fast by Day, a Feast must solemnize.
    Chorus. Io to *Hymen*; *Paeans* sing,
        To *Hymen*, and my *Muses* King.

Dinner

The Board being spread, furnish't with various
    Plenties:
The Brides faire Object in the Middle plac'd;
While she drinks Nectar, eates Ambrosiall dainties,
And like a Goddesse is admir'd and grac'd:
    Bacchus and *Ceres* fill their veines;
    Each Heart begins to ope a vent;

220

And now the *Healths* goe round;
    Their Bloods are warm'd; chear'd are their
      Braines
    All doe applaud their Loves Consent;
    So Love with Cheare is crown'd.
Let sensuall soules joy in full Bowles, sweet Dishes;
True Hearts, and Tongues, accord in joyful wishes.
    Chorus. Io to *Hymen*, &c.

After-Noone Musicke

Now whiles slow Howres doe feede the Times delay,
Confus'd discourse, with Musicke mixt among,
Fills up the semy-circle of the Day;
Now drawes the date our Lovers wish'd so long.
        Supper.
    A bounteous Hand the Board hath spred;
    Lyeus stirres so their Bloods a-new;
        All Joviall full of cheare;
        Sunne set.
    But *Phoebus* see, is gone to Bed;
    Loe *Hesperus* appeares in view,
        And twinckles in his sphere.
Now *ne plus ultra*; end, as you begin;
Yee waste good Howres; Time lost in Love, is sin.
    Chorus. Io to *Hymen*, &c.

Breake off your Complement; Musick, be dombe.
And pull your Cases o're your Fiddles eares;
Cry not, a Hall, a Hall; but Chamber-roome;
Dancing is lame; Youth's old at twentie yeares.

Going to Bed

Matrons; yee know what followes next;
Conduct the shame-fac'd Bride to Bed,
    (Though to her little rest)
Yee well can comment on the Text,

And, in Loves learning deeply read,
    Advise, and teach the best.
Forward's the Word; Y' are all so in this Arrant;
Wives give the Word; their Husbands give the
        Warrant.
    Chorus. Io to Hymen, &c.

Modestie in the Bride

Now droopes our Bride, and in her Virgin state,
Seemes like *Electra* 'mongst the Pleyades;
So shrinkes a Mayde when her Herculean Mate
Must plucke the fruite in her Hesperides.
    As she's a Bride, she glorious shines,
      Like *Cynthia,* from the Sunnes bright Sphere,
        Attracting all mens Eyes;
    But as she's Virgin, waines, and pines,
      As to the Man she approcheth neere;
        So Mayden glory dies.
But Virgin Beames no reall brightnesse render;
If they doe shine, in darke they shew their splendor.
    Chorus. Io to Hymen, &c.

Then let the darke Foyle of the Geniall Bed
Extend her brightnesse to his inward sight,
And by his sence he will be easly led
To know her vertue, by the absent light.
         Bride Points.
    Youth's; take his Poynts; your wonted right;
         Garters.
    And Maydens; take your due, her Garters;
      Take hence the Lights; begone;
    Love calls to Armes, Duell his Fight;
    Then all remove out of his Quarters,
      And leave them both alone:
That with substantiall heate, they may embrace,
And know Loves Essence, with his outward grace.
    Chorus. Io to Hymen, &c.

Hence Jealousie, Rivall to Loves delight;
Sowe not thy seede of strife in these two Harts;
May never cold affect, or spleenefull spight,
Confound this Musicke of agreeing parts;
    But Time (that steales the virtuall heate
    Where Nature keepes the vitall fire)
       (My Heart speakes in my Tongue)
    Supply with Fewell Lifes chiefe seate,
    Through the strong fervour of Desire:
       Love, living; and live long.
And ev'n as Thunder riseth gainst the Winde;
So may yee fight with Age; and conquer Kinde.
    Chorus. *Io* to *Hymen*: *Pæans* sing
       To *Hymen*, and my *Muses* King.

Christopher Brooke

NOTES
AND INDEXES

NOTES

Page 1. *The Sheepheard to his chosen Nimph. S. Phil. Sidney.* This is the Fourth Song from Sidney's *Astrophel and Stella,* first published in 4to, in 1591. For the texts of Sidney's writings used by Ling see *The Complete Works of Sir Philip Sidney* edited by A. Feuillerat (3 vols., 1922–3) and Rollins's notes to his edition of *E.H.*

Page 3. Theorello *A Sheepheards Edillion. E. B.* Brydges and Bullen agree in assigning the initials E. B. to Edmund Bolton, whose name is subscribed in full to a poem on p. 17. Bolton, the author of *The Elements of Armories* 1610, was an historian and poet who in 1617 formulated a scheme for a royal academy of letters and science.

Page 7. Astrophels *Love is dead. Sir Phil. Sidney.* From the poems appended to the third edition of Sidney's *Arcadia* 1598. 'Probably written on the occasion of Stella's (Lady Penelope Devereux') marriage.' *Bullen.*

Page 8. *A Palinode. E. B.* Edmund Bolton. See Note to page 3 (*Theorello*).

Page 9. Astrophell *the Sheep-heard, his complaint to his flocke. S. Phil. Sidney.* This is the Ninth Song from *Astrophel and Stella* 1591.

Page 11. Hobbinolls *Dittie in prayse of* Eliza etc. *Edm. Spencer.* From the April Æglogue of *The Shepheardes Calender* 1579. Five editions of the *S.C.* were published before 1600. The *E.H.* text is from the edition of 1597 (Rollins).

Page 15. *The Sheepheards* Daffadill. *Michaell Drayton.* First printed in *E.H.* Subsequently reprinted as part of *The ninth Eglog* in Drayton's *Poemes Lyrick and pastorall* [1605] and collected *Poems* 1619. Five of Drayton's poems were printed for the first time in *E.H.* See *The Works of Michael Drayton* edited by J. W. Hebel; Vol. V (1941) by Kathleen Tillotson, p. xxiii.

Page 17. *A Canzon Pastorall in honour of her Majestie. Edmund Bolton.* See Note to page 3 (*Theorello*).

Page 18. Melicertus *Madrigale. Ro. Greene.* Printed under the same title in Greene's *Menaphon* 1589 (second edition 1610). Greene's poems were printed in *The Plays and Poems of Robert Greene* edited by J. Churton Collins 1905.

Page 19. *Olde* Damons *Pastorall. Thom. Lodge.* This poem has not been found in any earlier volume than *E.H.* The four lines beginning *Golden cups* are quoted in *Englands Parnassus* (244), edited by C. Crawford 1913, above the signature D. Lodge.

Page 20. Perigot *and* Cuddies *Roundelay. Edm. Spencer.* From the August *Æglogue* of the *Shepheardes Calender* 1579. In *S.C.* the poem is printed as a dialogue in alternate lines between Perigot and Willye.

Page 23. Phillida *and* Coridon. *N. Breton.* First printed in *The Honorable Entertainement gieven to the Queenes Majestie in Progresse, at Eluetham in Hampshire, by the Right Honorable the Earle of Hertford,* 1591, under the title of *The Plowmans Song.* In the third edition, also dated 1591, the title is changed to *The Three Mens Song, sung the third morning under hir Majesties Gallerie window.* 'On Wednesday morning, about nine of the clock, as her Majestie opened a casement of her gallerie window, there were three excellent Musitians, who, being disguised in auncient countrey attire, did greet her with a pleasant song of Coridon and Phyllida, made in three parts of purpose. The song, as well for the worth of the Dittie, as for the aptnes of the note thereto applied, it pleased her Highnesse, after it had beene once sung, to command it againe, and highly to grace it with her chearefull acceptance and commendation. Mr R. W. Bond in the Clarendon Press edition of Lyly's Works 1902 claimed *The Entertainement* in the maine as Lyly's, but there is no external evidence in support of the claim, which has not been established. Mr Bond thought this poem was 'probably' Breton's. Apart from its ascription to him in *E.H.* there is the evidence of the Rawlinson MS. Poet. 85 fol. 3, where it is signed 'Britton.' It is included among other poems of Breton's in a manuscript which belonged to the late Mr F. W. Cosens from which Grosart printed several poems in his edition of Breton's Works 1879. It was reprinted in East's *Madrigales to* 3, 4 and 5 *parts* 1604.

Page 24. *To* Colin Cloute. *Sheepheard Tonie*. There are seven poems in *E.H.* attributed to 'Sheepheard Tonie.' The pseudonym most probably represents Antony Munday, although this cannot be absolutely established. There has been a good deal of controversy on the subject, and it is only possible here to summarize the arguments. The question has been fully dealt with in *The Library* N.S. Vol. I, No. 4, 1921, and Vol. IV, No. 1, 1923, and in *The Modern Language Review* Vol. XV, No. 4, 1920, by Miss M. St. Clare Byrne, and it is to her articles that I am principally indebted for the most recent light on the subject.

No serious claim to the authorship of the poems has been put forward on behalf of any other known writer, and although, no doubt, the general level of Munday's verse is greatly below that of 'Beautie sate bathing by a Spring,' passages from his acknowledged work can be selected, as Miss Byrne has pointed out, which would allow of the possibility of his having been the author of this famous lyric and which have points of resemblance with the 'Sheepheard Tonie' poems generally.

Webbe refers to Munday in his *Discourse of Eng-*

lish Poetrie 1586 as 'an earnest traveller in this arte, and in whose name I have seene very excellent workes, among which, surely, the most exquisite vaine of a witty poeticall heade is shewed in the sweete sobs of Sheepheardes and Nymphes; a worke well worthy to be viewed, and to bee esteemed as very rare Poetrie.' The book to which Webbe refers has disappeared, but the passage shows that Munday wrote pastoral poetry. It also establishes the fact of his contemporary reputation and makes it likely that poems by him would be included in *E.H.*, this likelihood being increased by the fact of Munday's acquaintance with Bodenham, whom he addresses in *Bel-vedére* as 'his looving and approved good friend.' Whilst, therefore, there is nothing to put Munday's claim out of court, there is the following evidence in his favour:

The poem here entitled *To Colin Cloute* is found in Book II, chap. 27, of his prose-romance *Primaleon of Greece* 1619,[1] and this fact, first discovered by Bullen, led him definitely to accept the theory that Munday was its author, an idea which he had before scouted on the ground of the mediocrity of his hitherto known verse. Sir H. Thomas has put forward the view that Munday 'incorporated into his text a popular poem of the day,' but whilst this is quite possible—he has with good reason been suspected of borrowing another's work in the case of Bk. II of *Amadis de Gaule*, published under his name—Sir Henry is not able to establish the fact of the theft in this instance.

Another poem in *E.H.*, *Montana the Sheepheard*, etc., p. 109, was first printed in *Fedele and Fortunio or Two Italian Gentlemen*, 1585, a play—in reality a translation of Pasqualigo's *Il Fedele*—about the authorship of which there has been much discussion.

[1] According to Esdaile's *List of English Tales & Romances* 1912, Book II was first printed in 1596, but I have not seen this edition.

Two perfect copies of this play exist. In one of them there is a dedicatory epistle addressed to M.R. and signed M. A., whilst in the other the epistle is addressed to John Heardson and signed A. M. Apart from the evidence afforded by the initials, Miss Byrne has given cogent reasons for attributing the work to Munday, although Sir E. K. Chambers has suggested that the wording of the epistle does not at first sight point to A. M. being himself the translator.

The last two lines of the second stanza of *Montana the Sheepheard* occur in a short passage printed in *Englands Parnassus* 1600 over the signature S. G. whilst four more lines of the play are there ascribed to Chapman; but the latter attribution is discredited, and *Englands Parnassus* is not, in any case, a reliable authority in these matters.

It will be seen, therefore, that although there is no one piece of evidence which establishes Munday's authorship of the 'Sheepheard Tonie' poems, there are a good many circumstances which, taken together, point very strongly to that conclusion.

Page 24. Rowlands *Song in praise of the fairest* Beta. *Mich. Drayton*. This poem, the only one of Drayton's in *E.H.* which was not there printed for the first time, had originally appeared in *Idea, the Shepheards Garland* 1593. Dr Hebel has pointed out, as evidence of the compiler of *E.H.* having had access to Drayton's manuscript, that the offensive reference to Roman Catholicism at the end of the 1593 version had already given place to the line found in the poem when it reappears in *Poemes Lyrick and pastorall* [1606] amd *Poems* 1619, where, however, it differs throughout from the *S.G.* and *E.H.* version.

Page 28. *The Barginet of* Antimachus. *Thom. Lodge*. This poem of Lodge's has not been traced to any earlier source.

Page 30. Menaphons *Roundelay*. *Ro. Greene*. From Greene's *Menaphon* 1589. See note to *Melicertus*

Medrigale p. 18. *Menaphon* was reprinted by E. Arber 1880 (The English Scholar's Library).

Page 31. *A Pastorall of* Phillis *and* Coridon. *N. Breton*. Probably from *The Arbor of Amorous Devices* etc. by *N. B. Gent*, 4to, 1597, a unique copy of which is preserved in the Capell Collection, Trinity College, Cambridge. Although *The A. of A.D.* is ascribed to Breton on the title-page, Richard Jones, the publisher, states in his address *To the Gentlemen Readers* that the book is 'many mens workes excellent Poets.' This poem is probably one of Breton's. It is in *Brittons Bowre of Delights* 1591 and 1597. The 1591 edition was edited by H. E. Rollins in 1933. *The A. of A.D.* is included in A. B. Grosart's edition of Breton (2 vols. 1879).

Grosart printed the following additional verse from the Cosens MS.:

> Make him live that dying longe
> Never durst for comfort seeke;
> Thou shalt heare so sweete a songe
> Never shepperde sounge the like.

Page 32. Coridon *and* Melampus *Song. Geo. Peele*. From a lost Pastoral by George Peele, *The Huntinge of Cupid*, licensed in 1591. Drummond, in 1609, read it and made extracts which are preserved among his MSS. at Edinburgh. Ten lines are printed in *Englands Parnassus* (979). See W. W. Greg, The Malone Society *Collections*, parts iv and v (1911).

Page 32. Tityrus *to his faire* Phillis. *J. D.* Brydges suggested that J. D. stood for Sir John Davies, and J. Davis is the signature in the Davison MS., but Bullen discovered this poem and the two following, signed J. M., in a volume by John Dickenson entitled *The Shepheardes Complaint, a Passionate Eclogue, written in English hexameters: whereunto are annexed other conceits, brieflie expressing the effect of Loves impressions*, etc., 4to, c. 1595, edited by A. B. Grosart

1878. The only known copy of the book was found at Lamport Hall. It passed to the Britwell Court collection and from thence to America in 1922.

Page 33. *Sheepheard. J. M.* See Note to preceding poem.

Page 33. *Another of the same Authour. J. M.* See above.

Page 35. Menaphon *to* Pesana. *Ro. Greene.* From Greene's *Menaphon* 1589.

Page 35. *A sweete Pastorall. N. Breton.* From *Brittons Bowre of Delights Contayning Many, most delectable and fine devices of rare Epitaphes, pleasant Poems, Pastorals and Sonets by N. B. Gent,* 4to, 1591, reprinted in 1597. Richard Jones, who issued this volume, refers, in his address to the reader, to the 'Authors absence' at the time of publication, and in fact in the following year, 1592, Nicholas Breton in his prefatory note to his *Pilgrimage to Paradise* states, 'Gentlemen there hath beene of late printed in London by one Richard Joanes, a printer a booke of english verses, entituled *Bretons bower of delights:* I protest it was donne altogether without my consent or knowledge; and many thinges of other mens mingled with few of mine, for except *Amoris Lachrimae:* an epitaphe upon Sir Phillip Sidney, and one or two other toies, which I know not how he unhappily came by, I have no part with any of them and so I beseech yee assuredly believe.' This poem probably is one of the excepted 'toies.' See Rollins's edition, 1935.

Page 37. Harpalus *complaynt on* Phillidaes *love* etc. *L. T. Haward, Earle of Surrie.* From *Tottels Miscellany* 1557, where it is printed among *Poems by Uncertain Auctours* and is therefore presumably not by the Earl of Surrey. I have used Arber's reprint of the first and second editions for purposes of collation.

Page 40. *Another of the same subject,* etc. *Shep. Tonie.* See Note to page 24 (*To Colin Cloute*).

Page 44. *The Nimphes meeting their May Queene,* etc. *Tho. Watson.* This poem was sung by 'six virgins' before Elizabeth at *The first daies entertainement* at Eluetham. See Note to page 23 (*Phillida and Coridon*). Mr Bond thought proud meant 'prov'd.' It was reprinted in Pilkington's *First Booke of Songs or Ayres* 1605, the words 'O gracious King' being substituted for 'O beautious Queene.' E. Arber in his 'Thomas Watson' (English Reprints, 1870) does not question Watson's authorship of this poem.

Page 44. Colin Cloutes *mournfull Dittie for the death of* Astrophell. *Edm. Spencer*. From Spenser's *Astrophel, A Pastorall Elegie Upon the death of . . . Sir Philip Sidney*, in *Colin Clouts come home againe* 1595.

Page 45. Damætas *Jigge in praise of his Love. John Wootton.* John Wootton was believed by Brydges to be a half-brother of Sir Henry Wotton. See Isaak Walton's *Life of Sir Henry Wotton*, where Sir John is described as 'a Gentleman excellently accomplished both by learning and travel.'

Page 46. Montanus *praise of his faire* Phæbe. *Thom. Lodge.* From Lodge's *Rosalynde* 1590, reprinted in 1592 and 1598, and frequently afterwards. *Rosalynde* was edited by W. W. Greg in 1907 for the Shakespeare Library.

Page 48. *The complaint of* Thestilis *the forsaken Sheepheard. L. T. Howard, E. of Surrie.* From *Tottels Miscellany* 1557, where it is printed among poems by *Uncertain Auctours*, and is therefore presumably not by the Earl of Surrey.

Page 49. *To* Phillis *the faire Sheepheardesse. S. E. D.* Although attributed to Sir Edward Dyer in *E.H.* and in the Davison MS., this poem is Sonnet XV of Lodge's *Phillis* 1593.

Page 50. *The Sheepheard* Dorons *Jigge. Ro. Greene.* From Greene's *Menaphon* 1589.

Page 51. Astrophell *his Song of* Phillida *and* Coridon. *N. Breton.* Believed by Bullen to have been first printed in *E.H.* Originally signed *S. Phil. Sidney*, a slip was afterwards inserted with the signature

N. Breton. An Elizabethan copy, signed 'Britton,' is in MS. Rawlinson Poet. 85.

Page 53. *The passionate Sheepheards Song. W. Shakespeare.* From Act IV of *Love's Labour's Lost*, first published in 4to, in 1598. The poem was also printed in *The Passionate Pilgrime* 1599. *L.L.L.* has these two additional lines after the line: 'youth so apt to pluck at sweet':

> Doe not call it sinne in me,
> That I am forsworne for thee;

Page 54. *The unknowne Sheepheards complaint. Ignoto.* First printed in Weelkes *Madrigals To* 3, 4, 5 and 6 *voyces* 1597, and again in *The Passionate Pilgrime* 1599, from which volume the version in *E.H.* was probably taken. Bullen and Sir Sidney Lee agree in attributing this poem to R. Barnfield on the ground that the poem following, undoubtedly by him, is headed *Another of the same Sheepheards*. Both poems are anonymous in *The Passionate Pilgrim*. The heading of the poem which follows in *E.H.* hardly constitutes evidence of the authorship of this poem.

Page 55. *Another of the same Sheepheards. Ignoto.* From *Poems: In divers humors*, part of a volume entitled *The Encomion of Lady Pecunia* 1598 by Richard Barnfield. The poem was also printed in *The Passionate Pilgrime* 1599. Thirty lines have been omitted from the poem as it is printed in *P.I.D.H.* and *P.P.*, and a new terminal couplet substituted. Sir Sidney Lee suggests (*The Passionate Pilgrim*, Facsimile of the First Edition; Clarendon Press 1905) that the compiler of *E.H.* was making use of an independent manuscript source, but I think it likely that the poem was taken from *P.P.*, as the two preceding poems are found in that volume, and that the thirty lines were omitted by the editor of *E.H.* on account of their non-pastoral nature. Barnfield's poems were edited by A. B. Grosart (1876) and were included in

E. Arber's *The English Scholar's Library*, 1882. They have recently been reprinted by M. Summers (the Fortune Press n.d.).

Page 56. *The Sheepheards allusion of his owne amorous infelicitie*, etc. *Tho. Watson.* This poem is Sonnet VIII of T. Watson's *Hecatompathia* c. 1582, included in E. Arber's *English Reprints* 1870.

Page 57. Montanus *Sonnet to his faire* Phæbe. *Thom. Lodge.* From Lodge's *Rosalynde* 1590.

Page 58. Phæbes *Sonnet, a replie* to Montanus *passion. Thom. Lodge.* From Lodge's *Rosalynde* 1590.

Page 59. Coridons *supplication to* Phillis. *N. Breton.* From *Brittons Bowre of Delights* 1591, reprinted in 1597.

Page 60. Damætas *Madrigall in praise of his* Daphnis. *J. Wootton.* See Note to page 45 (*Damætus Jigge*).

Page 62. Dorons *description of his faire Sheepheardesse* Samela. *Ro. Greene.* From Greene's *Menaphon* 1589.

Page 63. Wodenfrides *Song in praise of* Amargana. *W. H.* W. H. may stand for William Hunnis, several of whose poems are printed in *The Paradyse of Dainty Devises* 1576 edited by H. E. Rollins, 1927.

Page 64. *Another of the same. W. H.* See preceding Note.

Page 66. *An excellent Pastorall Dittie. Shep. Tonie.* See Note to page 24 (*To Colin Cloute*).

Page 68. Phillidaes *Love-call to her* Coridon, *and his replying. Ignoto.* This poem has been claimed for Raleigh on the ground that it is signed *Ignoto*, a pseudonym which was supposed by Warton and others to designate this author. This was certainly not always the case, and there is no other evidence in support of the claim in this instance. It is not included even among the doubtful poems by Agnes M. C. Latham in her edition of *Poems of Sir Walter Raleigh*, 1929.

Page 70. *The Sheepheards solace. Tho. Watson.* Sonnet XCII of Watson's *Hecatompathia* c. 1582.

Page 70. Syrenus *Song to* Eugerius. *Bar. Yong*. From Bartholomew Yong's (or Young's) translation of Montemayor's Spanish Romance *Diana*, published in 1598, but finished in manuscript, as he tells us, fifteen years earlier. *Diana* has not been reprinted.

Page 73. *The Sheepheard* Arsileus *replie to* Syrenus *Song. Bar. Yong*. From Yong's *Diana* 1598.

Page 76. *A Sheepheards dreame. N. Breton*. From *Brittons Bowre of Delights* 1591. Second edition 1596.

Page 77. *The Sheepheards Ode. Rich. Barnefielde*. From Barnfield's *Cynthia. With Certaine Sonnets*, etc. 1595.

Page 79. *The Sheepheards commendation of his Nimph. Earle of Oxenford*. Printed in *The Phœnix Nest* 1593 (edited by Hugh Macdonald, 1926 and H. E. Rollins, 1931) where it is signed E.O. Poems by Edward Vere, Earl of Oxford, occur in *The Paradise of Dainty Devises* and other contemporary miscellanies and manuscripts. Hannah in his *Courtly Poets* ascribes twenty-one poems to him, but this number includes two poems wrongly attributed to him in *Englands Parnassus*.

Page 81. Coridon *to his* Phillis. *S. E. Dyer*. Printed anonymously in *The Phœnix Nest* 1593. It is ascribed to Dyer in the Davison MS.

Page 82. *The Sheepheards description of Love. Ignoto*. Printed anonymously in *The Phœnix Nest* 1593. Originally signed S. W. R. in *E.H.*, a slip *Ignoto* was substituted. It is ascribed to S. W. Rawley in the Davison MS. and is printed anonymously in *Davisons Poetical Rapsody* 1602. Miss Latham does not attribute the poem to Raleigh.

Page 83. *To his Flocks. H. C.* The four poems in *E. H.*, signed H. C., were attributed to Henry Constable until Professor Rollins pointed out (*T.L.S.* 1 Oct. 1931) that this poem occurs in *Piers Plainnes seven years Prentiship* 1595, attributed to Henry Chettle. Sir E. K. Chambers (*Oxford Book of Sixteenth Cen-*

tury Verse 1932) remarks that the four poems must, no doubt, stand or fall together; but that the authorship of *Piers Plainnes* rests only on the initials H. C.

Page 84. *A Roundelay betweene two Sheepheards.* *Mich. Drayton.* First published in *E.H.* Reprinted as part of the *ninth Eglog of Poemes Lyrick and pastorall* [1606] and *Poems* 1619.

Page 85. *The solitarie Sheepheards Song. Thom. Lodge.* From Lodge's *A Margarite of America* 1596.

Page 85. *The Sheepheards resolution in love. Tho. Watson.* Sonnet XXXVII of Watson's *Hecatompathia* c. 1582.

Page 86. Coridons *Hymne in praise of* Amarillis. *T. B.* Brydges suggested that the initials T. B. stood for Thomas Bastard, from whose book *Chrestoleros, Seven bookes of Epigrames* 1598 there are eleven quotations in *Englands Parnassus.*

Page 87. *The Sheepheard* Carillo *his Song. Bar. Yong.* From Yong's *Diana* 1598.

Page 90. Corins *dreame of his faire* Chloris. *W. S.* Sonnet XIII of William Smith's *Chloris, or The Complaint of the passionate despised Shepheard* 1596. See Sir S. Lee's *Elizabethan Sonnets* 1904, II, 331.

Page 91. *The Sheepheard* Damons *passion. Thom. Lodge.* Sonnet XII of Lodge's *Phillis* 1593. See Sir S. Lee's *Elizabethan Sonnets* II, 8.

Page 91. *The Sheepheard* Musidorus *his complaint. S. Phil. Sidney.* From Sidney's *Arcadia* 1590.

Page 92. *The Sheepheards braule, one halfe aunswering the other. S. Phil. Sidney.* From Sidney's *Arcadia* 1590.

Page 92. Dorus *his comparisons. S. Phil. Sidney.* From *Arcadia* 1590.

Page 93. *The Sheepheard* Faustus *his Song. Bar. Yong.* From Yong's *Diana* 1598.

Page 95. *Another of the same, by* Firmius *the Sheepheard. Bar. Yong.* From Yong's *Diana* 1598.

Page 96. Damelus *Song to his* Diaphenia. *H. C.* See Note to page 83 (*To his Flocks*).

Page 97. *The Sheepheard* Eurymachus *to his faire Sheepheardesse* Mirimida. *Ro. Greene.* From Greene's *Francescos Fortunes* 1590.

Page 99. *The Sheepheard* Firmius *his Song. Bar. Yong.* From Yong's *Diana* 1598.

Page 101. *The Sheepheards praise of his sacred* Diana. Printed anonymously in *The Phœnix Nest* 1593. In the Bodleian (Malone) copy of *E.H.* the poem is signed S. W. R., over which initials a slip *Ignoto* has been pasted. In the B.M. copy the signature has been erased and the slip is missing. In the Davison MS. it is ascribed to W. R. Hannah prints it among Raleigh's poems. Miss Latham prints it among Raleigh's doubtful poems.

Page 102. *The Sheepheards dumpe. S. E. D.* Printed in *The Phœnix Nest* 1593, where it is attributed to T. L. Gent., i.e. Thomas Lodge. It is printed again, with some variations, on page 198 where it is signed *Ignoto*. The Davison MS. gives it to E. Dier.

Page 103. *The Nimph* Dianæs *Song. Bar. Yong.* From Yong's *Diana* 1598.

Page 105. Rowlands *Madrigall. Mich. Drayton.* Printed for the first and only time in *E.H.* See J. W. Hebel's *Drayton* I (1931), 495–496.

Page 107. Alanius *the Sheepheard, his dolefull Song*, etc. *Bar. Yong.* From Yong's *Diana* 1598. Versions of four of Montemayor's poems, included in *E.H.*, are given in a translation of *Diana* made by Sir T. Wilson, of which the first book—all that remains—was printed by Sir H. Thomas in *Revue Hispanique* (1920). See Rollins's note to this poem.

Page 109. Montana *the Sheepheard, his love* to Aminta. *Shep. Tonie.* First printed in *Fedele and Fortunio or Two Italian Gentlemen*. See Note to page 24 (*To Colin Cloute*).

Page 109. *The Sheepheards sorrow for his* Phæbes *dis-*

daine. Ignoto. **Originally signed M. F. G., i.e. Fulke**
Greville, a slip *Ignoto* was substituted. In *E.H.* 1614
the poem is signed I. F. and in the Davison MS. it is
attributed to 'F. Grevill.' It is not printed in Fulke
Greville's *Workes* 1633. The authorship of the
'M. F. G.' poems is not discussed in G. Bullough's
Poems and Dramas of Fulke Greville [1938].
Neither this poem nor 'Old Melibeous Song' can be
attributed to him on any evidence. This poem is
signed T. L. Gent in *The Phœnix Nest* 1593.

Page 111. Espilus *and* Therion, *their contention in song
for the May-Ladie. S. Phil. Sidney.* From Sidney's
Lady of May, first published in the third edition of
Arcadia 1598.

Page 112. *Olde* Melibeus *Song, courting his Nimph.
Ignoto.* Originally signed M. F. G., a slip *Ignoto* was
substituted. In *E.H.* 1614 the poem is unsigned. It is
assigned to F. Grevill in the Davison MS. It is not
included in his *Workes* 1633.

Page 113. *The Sheepheard* Sylvanus *his Song. Bar.
Yong.* From Yong's *Diana* 1598.

Page 113. Coridons *Song. Thom. Lodge.* From Lodge's
Rosalynde 1590.

Page 115. *The Sheepheards Sonnet. Rich. Barnefielde.*
This poem is Sonnet XV of Barnfield's *Cynthia* 1595.

Page 116. Selvagia *and* Silvanus *their song to* Diana.
Bar. Yong. From Yong's *Diana* 1598.

Page 117. Montanus *his Madrigall. Ro. Greene.* From
Greene's *Francescos Fortunes* 1590.

Page 119. Astrophell *to* Stella, *his third Song. S. Phil.
Sidney.* From *Astrophel* and *Stella* 1591.

Page 120. *A Song betweene* Syrenus *and* Sylvanus. *Bar.
Yong.* From Yong's *Diana* 1598.

Page 122. Ceres *Song in emulation of* Cinthia. From
*Speeches Delivered To Her Majestie This Last Pro-
gresse, At The Right Honorable the Lady Russels at
Bissam, the Right Honorable the Lorde Chandos, at
Sudley* (i.e. Sudeley), etc. Oxford, 1592. The Speeches

in this 'Entertainement' are claimed by Mr R. W.
Bond for Lyly, who may have written the poem.
There is, however, no external evidence for this, and
Lyly's authorship of the lyrics in his genuine plays
has been questioned.

Page 123. *A Pastorall Ode to an honourable friend.*
E. B. Probably Edmund Bolton. See Note to page 3
(*Theorello*).

Page 124. *A Nimphs disdaine of Love. Ignoto.* R. W.
Bond includes this poem in his edition of Lyly but
without any evidence.

Page 125. *Apollos Love-Song for faire* Daphne. From
the *Speeches Delivered to Her Majestie* etc. *at Sudley*
etc. 1592. See Note to page 122 (*Ceres Song*).

Page 125. *The Sheepheard* Delicius *his Dittie. Bar.*
Yong. From Yong's *Diana* 1598.

Page 127. Amintas *for his* Phillis. *Tho. Watson.* From
The Phœnix Nest 1593, where it is signed T. W. Gent.

Page 130. Faustus *and* Firmius *sing to their Nimph by*
turnes. Bar. Yong. From Yong's *Diana* 1598.

Page 131. Sireno *a Sheepheard, having a lock of his*
faire Nimphs haire, etc. S. Phil. Sidney. From the
poems appended to the third edition of *Arcadia* 1598.

Page 133. *A Song betweene* Taurisius *and* Diana,
aunswering verse for verse. Bar. Yong. From Yong's
Diana 1598.

Page 134. *Another Song before her Majestie at Oxford,*
sung by a comely Sheepheard, etc. Anonimus. From
The Entertainement at Sudeley 1592. See Note to
page 122 (*Ceres Song*).

Page 135. *The Sheepheards Song: a Caroll or Himne*
for Christmas. E. B. Probably by Edmund Bolton.
See Note to page 3 (*Theorello*).

Page 136. Arsileus *his Caroll, for joy of the new mari-*
age, etc. Bar. Yong. From Yong's *Diana* 1598.

Page 139. Philistus *farewell to false* Clorinda. *Out of*
M. Morleyes *Madrigalls.* From *Thomas Morleys*
Madrigalls to Foure Voyces . . . the First Booke 1594.

As in the case of practically all the poems in *E.H.* taken from the Song Books the author has not been identified.

Page 139. Rosalindes *Madrigall. Thom. Lodge.* From Lodge's *Rosalynde* 1590.

Page 141. *A Dialogue Song betweene* Sylvanus *and* Arsilius. *Bar. Yong.* From Yong's *Diana* 1598.

Page 142. Montanus *Sonnet. S. E. D.* This poem, ascribed to Sir Edward Dyer, is printed in Lodge's *Rosalynde* and is no doubt by Lodge.

Page 143. *The Nimph* Selvagia *her Song. Bar. Yong.* From Yong's *Diana* 1598.

Page 144. *The Heard-mans happie life. Out of M.* Birds *set Songs.* From William Byrd's *Psalmes, Sonets & Songs,* etc., 1588.

Page 145. Cinthia *the Nimph, her Song to faire* Polydora. *Bar. Yong.* From Yong's *Diana* 1598.

Page 147. *The Sheepheard to the flowers. Ignoto.* Printed anonymously in *The Phœnix Nest* 1593. It is included by Hannah among Raleigh's poems, but there seems to be no authority for ascribing it to him.

Page 149. *The Sheepheard* Arsilius, *his Song to his Rebeck. Bar. Yong.* From Yong's *Diana* 1598.

Page 151. *Another of* Astrophell *to his* Stella. *S. Phil. Sidney.* The eighth song from *Astrophel and Stella* 1591. The text is from the *Arcadia* 1598. The poem as published in 1591 is shorter.

Page 154. Syrenus *his Song to* Dianaes *Flocks. Bar. Yong.* From Yong's *Diana* 1598.

Page 155. *To* Amarillis. *Out of M.* Birds *set Songs.* From William Byrd's *Psalmes, Sonets & Songs,* etc., 1588.

Page 156. Cardenia *the Nimph, to her false Sheepheard* Faustus. *Bar. Yong.* From Yong's *Diana* 1598.

Page 158. *Of* Phillida. *Out of M.* Bird's *set Songs.* From William Byrd's *Psalmes, Sonets & Songs* 1588.

Page 159. Melisea *her Song, in scorne of her Sheepheard* Narcissus. *Bar. Yong.* From Yong's *Diana* 1598.

Page 159. *His aunswere to the Nimphs Song. Bar. Yong.* From Yong's *Diana* 1598.

Page 160. *Her present aunswere againe to him. Bar. Yong.* From Yong's *Diana* 1598.

Page 161. *His last replie. Bar. Yong.* From Yong's *Diana* 1598.

Page 162. Philon *the Sheepheard, his Song. Out of M.* Birds *set Songs.* From William Byrd's *Songs of Sundrie Natures* 1589.

Page 163. Lycoris *the Nimph, her sad Song. Out of M.* Morleyes *Madrigalls.* From Thomas Morley's *Madrigalls to Foure Voyces . . . the First Booke* 1594.

Page 163. *To his Flocks.* From John Dowland's *First Booke of Songes or Ayres of foure partes,* etc. 1597.

Page 164. *To his Love.* From John Dowland's *First Booke of Songes,* etc. 1597.

Page 165. *Another of his* Cinthia. Printed in John Dowland's *First Booke of Songes,* etc. 1597. The poem is Sonnet LI of *Cælica* in Greville's *Certaine Learned and Elegant Workes* 1633 (Sonnet LII of G. Bullough's *Fulke Greville*). Sonnet V of *Cælica* was also printed in Dowland's *First Booke of Songes.*

Page 166. *Another to his* Cinthia. Printed in John Dowland's *First Booke of Songes,* etc. 1597. It is ascribed to 'The Earle of Cumberland' in the Davison MS. This would presumably be George Clifford, third Earl of Cumberland (1558–1605). Dr Fellowes (*English Madrigal Verse*) states that the initials W. S. have been found attached to an early MS. copy of these lines.

Page 167. Montanus *Sonnet in the woods. S. E. D.* Though attributed to Sir Edward Dyer, this poem is taken from Lodge's *Rosalynde* 1590.

Page 168. *The Sheepheards sorrow, being disdained in love. Thom. Lodge.* From Lodge's *Phillis.* See Hunterian Club reprint, Vol. II. As the poem is not a sonnet it was not reprinted by Sir S. Lee. It was included in *The Phœnix Nest* 1593.

Page 171. *A Pastorall Song betweene* Phillis *and* Amarillis, etc. *H. C.* See Note to page 83.

Page 173. *The Sheepheards Antheme. Mich. Drayton.* Printed in *E.H.* for the first time. It forms part of *The Second Eglog in Poemes Lyrick and pastorall* [1606] and *Poems* 1619.

Page 174. *The Countesse of Pembrookes Pastorall. Shep. Tonie.* See Note to page 24 (*To Colin Cloute*).

Page 176. *Another of* Astrophell. *S. Phil. Sidney.* From the Poems appended to the third edition of *Arcadia* 1598.

Page 177. *Faire* Phillis *and her Sheepheard. J. G.* Ritson suggested that the initials J. G. stood for John Gough. John Grange, the author of *The Golden Aphroditis* 1577, has also been suggested, but the poetry in this volume has little resemblance to *Fair* Phillis *and her Sheepheard.* Bullen considered that the verses were in Constable's manner.

Page 180. *The Sheepheards Song of* Venus *and* Adonis. *H. C.* See Note to page 83.

Page 184. Thirsis *the Sheepheard his deaths song. Out of Maister* N. Young *his* Musica Transalpina. From N. Yonge's *Musica Transalpina. Madrigals translated of foure, five and sixe parts chosen out of divers excellent Authors* 1588. In the place of lines 9, 10 and 11 *M.T.* gives the following:

Wherewith in haste to die he did betake him
Thinking it death that life would not forsake him.
And while his look full fixed he retained
On her eyes full of pleasure;

Page 185. *Another stanza added after. Out of the same.* From N. Yonge's *Musica Transalpina* 1588.

Page 185. *Another Sonet thence taken.* From N. Yonge's *Musica Transalpina* 1588.

Page 186. *The Sheepheards slumber. Ignoto.* This poem has been claimed for Raleigh, but only on the ground that it is signed *Ignoto* in *E.H.* See Note to page 68. Rollins calls attention to a copy (MS. Harleian 7392 f. 51) signed 'L. OX,' that is Lord Oxford.

Page 190. *In wonted walkes,* etc. *S. Phil. Sidney.* From the Poems appended to the third edition of *Arcadia* 1598. It had been previously printed as Sonnet VIII of Decade 3 in Constable's *Diana* 1594 (dated on t.p. 1584).

Page 190. *Of disdainfull* Daphne. *M. H. Nowell.* In *E.H.* 1614 the Poem is signed M. N. Howell. The Davison MS. gives H. Nowell. This cannot be Thomas Howell, the author of *H. His Devises,* the possibility of which was hinted at by Sir E. Brydges, as Howell's poetry is of an earlier character. C. Crawford (*Englands Parnassus,* Clarendon Press 1913) suggests Master Henry Noel, a courtier noted for his extravagant behaviour and wit. Rollins calls attention to a poem in MS. Rawlinson Poet. 85, f. 12 signed 'Mr Nowell,' and to a distich also signed 'Nowell' in another Rawlinson MS.

Page 192. *The passionate Sheepheard to his love. Chr. Marlow.* There are four versions of this famous poem. Stanzas 1, 2, 3 and 5 appeared in *The Passionate Pilgrime* 1599, where they are printed thus:

> Live with me and be my Love,
> And we will all the pleasures prove
> That hilles and vallies, dales and fields,
> And all the craggy mountaines yeeld.

> There will we sit upon the Rocks,
> And see the Shepheards feed their flocks,
> By shallow Rivers, by whose fals
> Melodious birds sing Madrigals.

> There will I make thee a bed of Roses,
> With a thousand fragrant poses,
> A cap of flowers, and a Kirtle
> Imbrodered all with leaves of Mirtle.

A belt of straw and Yvye buds,
With Corall Clasps and Amber studs,
And if these pleasures may thee move,
Then live with me, and be my Love.

The poem is printed in Walton's *Compleat Angler* 1653 under the title of *The Milkmaid's Song*—"twas that smooth song which was made by Kit Marlow, now at least fifty years ago'—and there is a manuscript version in the *Thornborough Commonplace Book*. (See Mr Ingram's *Christopher Marlowe and his Associates*, 1904, pp. 222, 225.)

In the MS. verses 4 and 5 are transposed and are followed by an extra verse:

Thy dyshes shal be filde with meate
Suche as the gods doe use to eate
Shall one and everye table bee
preparde each day for thee and me

which with some variations appears again in the second edition of *The Compleat Angler*. These lines have not been accepted as Marlowe's.

Page 193. *The Nimphs reply to the Sheepheard. Ignoto.* Bullen states that this poem was originally signed S. W. R. in the extant copies and that a slip *Ignoto* was substituted. This is not the case with the B.M., the John Rylands or Bodleian copies, all of which have the signature *Ignoto* and no slip. In the John Rylands copy the signature *Ignoto* is followed by a manuscript note in a contemporary hand: 'alias Sʳ Walt. Ralegh.' The first stanza was printed anonymously in *The Passionate Pilgrime* 1599 as *Loves aunswere* to the four stanzas of Marlowe's poem. The whole poem is given in *The Compleat Angler* 1653 as 'made by Sir Walter Raleigh in his younger dayes.' In the second edition of *The Compleat Angler* another stanza was added. Miss Latham includes this poem among Raleigh's authentic poems.

Page 194. *Another of the same nature, made since. Ignoto.* The author of this version of the poem has not been identified.

Page 195. *The Wood-mans walke. Shep. Tonie.* See Note to page 24 (*To Colin Cloute*).

Page 198. Thirsis *the Sheepheard, to his Pipe. Ignoto.* In *The Phœnix Nest* 1593 it is signed 'T.L. gent.' See Note to page 102 (*The Sheepheards dumpe*).

Page 199. An excellent Sonnet of a Nimph. *S. Phil. Sidney.* Bullen thought this poem was first printed in *E.H.*, but it is in the second edition of *Arcadia* 1593. See *Feuillerat* II, 53.

Page 199. *A Report Song in a dreame, between a Sheepheard and his Nimph. N. Breton.* Appeared in *E.H.* for the first time according to Grosart.

Page 200. *Another of the same. N. Breton.* Appeared in *E.H.* for the first time according to Grosart.

Page 201. *The Sheepheards conceite of* Prometheus. *S. E. D.* Presumably by Sir Edward Dyer. From the poems appended to the third edition of *Arcadia* 1598, where it is headed with the initials E. D.

Page 201. *Another of the same. S. Phil. Sidney.* This is Sidney's answer to the preceding poem.

Page 202. *The Sheepheards Sunne. Shep. Tonie.* See Note to page 24 (*To Colin Cloute*).

Page 204. Colin *the enamoured Sheepheard, singeth this passion of love. Geo. Peele.* From Peele's *Araygnement of Paris* 1584. There is a Malone Society reprint of this play.

Page 205. Oenones *complaint in blanke verse. Geo. Peele.* From Peele's *Araygnement of Paris* 1584. The meaning of the two first lines of the second stanza is obscure as they stand in *E.H.*

Page 206. *The Sheepheards Consort. Out of Ma. Morleys Madrigals.* From Thomas Morley's *Madrigals to four Voyces—First Booke* 1594.

NOTES ON THE ADDITIONAL POEMS
OF 1614

I have not, in my notes to the 1600 *edition, given the readings of the* 1614 *edition, as although it occasionally corrects the former it has presumably no independent authority.*

On the 20th December, 1613, John Flasket transferred his rights in *E.H.* to Richard More (*The Stationers Register* Arber iii, 538), who in the following year issued an octavo edition with nine poems added.

ENGLANDS
HELICON.
OR
THE MVSES
HARMONY.

LONDON:
Printed for RICHARD MORE, and are to
be sould at his Shop in S. Dunstanes
Church-yard. 1614.

Collation: [A]⁴, B-Q⁸, R⁴. The last leaf, which was doubtless a blank, is missing from the B.M. copy.

In the place of A.B's sonnet to Bodenham and his address to Wanton and Faucet, and Ling's address *To the Reader*, More substituted a dedicatory sonnet to Lady Elizabeth Cary:

TO THE TRULY
VERTUOUS AND
Honourable Lady, the Lady
ELIZABETH CARIE.

DEIGNE *worthy Lady*, (*Englands* happy *Muse*,
Learnings delight, that all things else exceeds)
To shield from *Envies* pawe and times abuse:
The tunefull noates of these our *Shepheards* reeds.

Sweet is the concord, and the *Musicke* such
That at it Rivers have been seen to daunce,
When these musitians did their sweet pipes tuch
In silence lay the vales, as in a traunce.

The *Satyre* stops his race to heare them sing,
And bright *Apollo* to these layes hath given
So great a gift, that any favouring
The *Shepheards* quill, shall with the lights of Heaven

    Have equall fate: Then cherrish these (faire
       Stem)
    So shall they live by thee, and thou by them.
           Your Honours
            ever to command
              RICHARD MORE.

Lady Cary was the wife of Sir Henry Cary, first Viscount Falkland, and the mother of Lucius Cary, second Lord Falkland. She was herself a woman of learning and a poet.

More added *The Table of all the Songs and Pastorals, with the Authors names, contained in this*

Booke. This *Table* I have not reprinted as it merely consists of the titles of the poems and the signatures appended to them in More's edition. In his attributions he follows Flasket's edition, as amended by the slips, and his *Table* practically corresponds to the headings to my notes except in the two instances mentioned therein.

The second edition appears to be at least as rare as the first. When the Britwell Court copy, formerly in the possession of Farmer, Steevens and Heber, was sold in March, 1924, Messrs Sotheby were able to trace the existence of only two others, the Corser copy, now in the British Museum, and the Roxburgh-Daniel-Huth copy, sold in 1913. See Rollins II, pp. 9–10.

Page 209. *An Invective against Love.* First published in *Davisons Poetical Rapsody* 1602, reprinted in 1608, 1611 and 1621. In the B.M. is a manuscript (Harl. MS. 280 fo. 102 et seq.) giving the first lines of a number of *Poems in Rhyme and Measured Verse by A. W.* This poem which follows *Another of* Astrophell (page 176 of this edition) in More's edition, is included in the list. The manuscript is believed to be in the handwriting of Francis Davison, but who A. W. is has never been discovered. W. T. Linton threw out the very reasonable suggestion that the initials might stand for Anonymous Writer. See *Davisons Poetical Rhapsody*, edited by A. H. Bullen, 1890. The 1611 edition of *D.P.R.* was used for the 1614 edition of *E.H.*

Page 210. *Dispraise of Love, and Lovers follies. Ignoto.* From *Davisons Poetical Rapsody.* Attributed to A. W. in Harl. MS. 280 fo. 102. In More's edition the poem follows *The Sheepheards Slumber* (page 186 of this edition).

Page 211. *Two Pastorals, upon three friends meeting. S. Phil. Sidney.* First published in *Davisons Poetical Rapsody*, where it is headed, in the first edition, *Two*

Pastorals made by Sir Philip Sidney never yet published, upon his meeting with his two worthy friends, and fellow Poets, Sir Edward Dier and M. Fulke Grevill. In More's edition the poem follows *Another of the same nature made since* (page 194 of this edition).

Page 213. *An Heroicall Poeme. Ignoto.* From *Davisons Poetical Rapsody.* It is attributed to A. W. in Harl. MS. 280 fo. 102. In More's edition the poem follows *Thirsis the Sheepheard to his Pipe* (page 198 of this edition).

Page 215. *The Lovers absence kils me, her presence kils me. Ignoto.* From *Davisons Poetical Rapsody.* It is attributed to A. W. in Harl. MS. 280 fo. 102), In More's edition the poem follows *Another of the same* (page 200 of this edition). This poem has no title in the first edition of *D.P.R.*

Page 216. *Love the only price of love. Ignoto.* From *Davisons Poetical Rapsody.* Attributed to A. W. in Harl. MS. 280 fo. 102. In More's edition the poem follows *.The Sheepheards Sunne* (page 202 of this edition).

Page 217. Thyrsis *praise of his Mistresse. W. Browne.* First printed in *E.H.* 1614. William Browne, the author of *Britannias Pastorals.* His *Poems* were edited by G. Goodwin (1893). This poem and the two following conclude More's edition.

Page 219. *A defiance to disdainefull Love. Ignoto.* From *Davisons Poetical Rapsody.* It is attributed to A. W. in Harl. MS. 280 fo. 102.

Page 219. An Epithalamium; or a Nuptiall Song, applied to the Ceremonies of Marriage. *Christopher Brooke.* First printed in *E.H.* 1614.

INDEX OF AUTHORS

As many of the attributions in *Englands Helicon* are doubtful, this index is merely a guide. The Notes at the end of the book must be consulted, especially for poems attributed to Dyer and Raleigh and Thomas Howard.

Anonymous, 37, 48, 122, 125, 134, 163, 209, *see also* Ignoto

T. B., 86

Barnfield, R., 54, 55, 77, 115

Bolton, E., 3, 8, 17, 123, 135

Breton, N., 23, 31, 35, 51, 59, 76, 199, 200

Brook, Lord (F. Greville), 109, 112, 165

Brooke, C., 219

Browne, W., 217

Byrd, W. (*Song Books*), 144, 155, 158, 162

C[hettle], H., 83, 96, 171, 180

Cumberland, Earl of, 166

D[ickenson], J., 32, 33, 33

Dowland, J. (*First Book of Songs or Airs*), 163, 164, 165, 166

Drayton, M., 15, 24, 84, 105, 173

Dyer, Sir E., 81, 102, 142, 167, 201

I. G., 177

Greene, R., 18, 30, 35, 50, 62, 97, 117

W. H[unnis], 63, 64

Ignoto, 54, 55, 68, 82, 101, 102, 109, 112, 124, 147, 186, 193, 194, 198, 210, 213, 215, 216, 219

Lodge, T., 19, 28, 46, 49, 57, 58, 85, 91, 102, 113, 139, 142, 167, 168, 198

I. M., *see* J. Dickenson

Marlowe, C., 192

Morley, T. (*Madrigals*), 139, 163, 206

Munday, A., *see* Sheepheard Tonie

Nowell, M. H., 190

Oxford, Earl of, 79

Peele, George, 32, 204, 205

Raleigh, Sir W., 68, 82, 101, 186, 193

W. S[mith], 90
Shakespeare, W., 53
Sheepheard Tonie, 24, 40, 66, 109, 174, 195, 202
Sidney, Sir P., 1, 7, 9, 91, 92, 92, 111, 119, 131, 151, 176, 190, 199, 201, 211

Spenser, E., 11, 20, 44
Surrey, Earl of, 37, 48

A. W., 209, 210, 213, 215, 216, 219
Watson, T., 44, 56, 70, 85, 127
Wootton, John, 45, 60

Yong, B., 70, 73, 87, 93, 95, 99, 103, 107, 113, 116, 120, 125, 130, 133, 136, 141, 143, 145, 149, 154, 156, 159, 159, 161
Young, N. (*Musica Transalpina*), 184, 185, 185

INDEX OF FIRST LINES

A Blithe and bonny Country-Lasse,   *page* 113
A carefull Nimph, with carelesse greefe opprest,   66
A Satyre once did runne away for dread,   201
A Sheepheard and a Sheepheardesse,   174
A Silly Sheepheard lately sate   76
A Turtle sate upon a leavelesse tree,   57
Actaeon lost in middle of his sport   56
Ah trees, why fall your leaves so fast?   91
Alas, how wander I amidst these woods,   167
Alas my hart, mine eye hath wronged thee,   81
Alas what pleasure now the pleasant Spring   17
All is not golde that shineth bright in show,   209
As I beheld, I saw a Heardman wilde,   158
As it fell upon a day,   55
As to the blooming prime,   123
As withereth the Primrose by the river,   8
Aurora now began to rise againe,   127
Aurora's Blush (the Ensigne of the Day)   219
Away with these selfe-loving-Lads,   165

Beautie sate bathing by a Spring,   24
Burst foorth my teares, assist my forward greefe   163

Clorinda false adiew, thy love torments me: 139
Come away, come sweet Love,   164
Come live with mee, and be my deere,   194
Come live with mee, and be my love,   192
Come Sheepheards weedes, become your Maisters
    minde,   91
Coridon, arise my *Coridon*,   68

Diaphenia like the Daffadown-dillie,   96
Downe a downe, thus *Phillis* sung,   58

Ecclipsed was our Sunne, *page* 93

Faire fields proud *Floraes* vaunt, why i'st you
    smile, 35
Faire in a morne, (ô fairest morne) 51
Faire Love rest thee heere, 105
Faire Nimphs, sit ye heere by me, 202
Faustus, if thou wilt reade from me 156
Feede on my Flocks securely, 83
Fie on the sleights that men devise, 171
Fields were over-spread with flowers, 33
From Fortunes frownes and change remov'd, 19

Goe my flocke, goe get yee hence, 9
Good Muse rock me a sleepe, 35
Gorbo, as thou cam'st this way 15

Happy Sheepheards sit and see, 64
Harke jollie Sheepheards, 206
Hearbs, words, and stones, all maladies have
    cured, 134
Hey downe a downe did *Dian* sing, 124

I pre-thee keepe my Kine for me 87
I see thee jolly Sheepheard merrie, 116
I serve *Aminta*, whiter then the snowe, 109
If all the world and love were young, 193
If *Jove* him-selfe be subject unto Love, 85
If Love be life, I long to die, 210
If *Orpheus* voyce had force to breathe such
    musiques love 119
If that the gentle winde 95
If to be lov'd it thee offend, 159
In a Groave most rich of shade, 151
In dewe of Roses, steeping her lovely cheekes, 163
In Pescod time, when Hound to horne, 186
In pride of youth, in midst of May, 28
In the merry moneth of May, 23
256

In wonted walkes, since wonted fancies
change,   *page* 190
It fell upon a holy-Eve,   20
It was a Vallie gawdie greene,   117

Jolly Sheepheard, Sheepheard on a hill   45
Joyne mates in mirth to me,   211

Let now each Meade with flowers be depainted,   136
Let now the goodly Spring-tide make us merrie,   70
Like desart Woods, with darksome shades
obscured,   102
Like Desert woods, with darksome shades
obscured,   198
Like to *Diana* in her Sommer weede,   62
Love in my bosome like a Bee,   139
Loves Queene long wayting for her true-Love,   112

Melampus, when will Love be void of feares?   32
Melpomene the Muse of tragicke songs,   205
Me thinks thou tak'st the worser way,   160
Muses helpe me, sorrow swarmeth,   168
My fairest *Ganimede* disdaine me not,   115
My Flocks feede not, my Ewes breede not,   54
My hart and tongue were twinnes, at once
conceaved   125
My life (young Sheepheardesse) for thee   113
My *Phillis* hath the morning Sunne,   49
My Sheepe are thoughts, which I both guide
and serve,   92
My thoughts are winged with hopes, my hopes
with love,   166
My wanton Muse that whilome wont to sing,   213

Neere to a bancke with Roses set about,   173
Neere to the River banks, with greene   145
Never a greater foe did Love disdaine,   125
Nights were short, and dayes were long,   77
257

No more (ô cruell Nimph,) now hast thou
    prayed   *page* 107
Now have I learn'd with much adoe at last,   219
Now Love and Fortune turne to me againe,   149

O Gentle Love, ungentle for thy deede,   204
O Let that time a thousand moneths endure,   73
O shadie Vales, ô faire enriched Meades,   85
O Thou silver Thames, ô clearest christall flood,   24
Oh Woods unto your walks my body hies   109
Of mine owne selfe I doo complaine,   130
On a day, (alack the day,)   53
On a goodly Sommers day,   40
On a hill that grac'd the plaine   217
On a hill there growes a flower,   31
Onely joy, now heere you are,   1

Passed contents, Oh what meane ye?   154
Phœbe sate sweete she sate,   46
Phœbus delights to view his Laurell tree,   70
Phillida was a faire mayde,   37
Praysed be *Dianaes* faire and harmelesse light,   101
Prometheus, when first from heaven hie,   201

Ring out your belles, let mourning shewes be
    spread,   7

Say that I should say, I love ye?   200
Shall I say that I love you,   190
Shall we goe daunce the hay? The hay?   199
Sheepheard, saw you not   177
Sheepheard, what's Love, I pray thee tell?   82
Sheepheard, who can passe such wrong,   143
Sheepheard, why doo'st thou hold thy peace?   141
Sheepheards give eare, and now be still   99
Sheepheards that wunt on pipes of Oaten reede,   44
Since thou to me wert so unkinde,   161
Sweete Musique, sweeter farre   135

Sweete *Phillis*, if a silly Swaine,   *page* 59
Sweete thrall, first step to Loves felicitie,   33
Sweete Violets (Loves Paradise) that spread   147
Swell *Ceres* now, for other Gods are shrinking,   122

Tell me thou gentle Sheepheards Swaine,   84
The cause why that thou doo'st denie   133
The fairest Pearles that Northerne Seas doe
    breed,   216
The frozen snake, opprest with heaped snow   215
The Nightingale so soone as Aprill bringeth   176
The silly Swaine whose love breedes discontent,   32
The Sunne the season in each thing   63
Thestilis a silly Swaine, when Love did him
    forsake,   48
Though *Amarillis* daunce in greene,   155
Through a faire Forrest as I went   195
Through the shrubs as I can crack,   50
Thirsis enjoyed the graces,   185
Thirsis to die desired,   184
Tune on my pipe the praises of my Love,   60
Tune up my voyce, a higher note I yeeld,   111

Venus faire did ride,   180
Vertue, beauty, and speach, did strike, wound,
    charme,   199

We love, and have our loves rewarded?   92
What are my Sheepe, without their wonted
    food?   18
What changes heere, ô haire,   131
What pleasure have great Princes,   144
What Sheepheard can expresse   79
What time bright *Titan* in the *Zenith* sat,   90
When *Flora* proud in pompe of all her flowers   97
When tender Ewes brought home with evenings
    Sun,   30
When that I poore soule was borne,   103
259

When the dogge   *page* 142
While that the Sunne with his beames hot,   162
Who hath of *Cupids* cates and dainties prayed,   120
With fragrant flowers we strew the way,   44
Would mine eyes were christall Fountaines,   86

Yee dainty Nimphs that in this blessed Brooke   11
You Sheepheards which on hillocks sit   3
Young Sheepheard turne a-side, and move   159

Zephirus brings the time that sweetly senteth   185